playing to win

ambition

courage

determination

hard work

drive

humour and charm

staying on track

confidence

communication

10 steps to

achieving

your goals

leadership

playing to

win

Karren Brady

With Leon Hickman

The successful woman's game plan

CAPSTONE

First published 2004 by
Capstone Publishing Limited (A Wiley Company)
The Atrium
Southern Gate
Chichester
West Sussex PO19 8SQ
http://www.wileyeurope.com

CIP catalogue records for this book are available from the British Library and the US Library of Congress

ISBN 1-84112-563-6

Typeset in Zapf Humanist 11/15pt by Sparks Computer Solutions Ltd
http://www.sparks.co.uk

Printed and bound by TJ International Ltd, Padstow, Cornwall

10 9 8 7 6 5 4 3 2 1

contents

introduction

Every day I meet capable, intelligent women of all ages in positions of responsibility, and yet the number appointed to boardrooms is very small. At the next level, the percentage of women who own or run a company is pitiful. Is there something wrong with us? Or something so exceptional about men that they are automatically promoted in front of women? I do not think so and, surely, only a Neanderthal chauvinist would answer those two questions with affirmatives.

But something is amiss. All the statistics say so. The Women and Equality Unit reported in 2003 that in all UK listed companies fewer than 1% of chairmen were women, and to emphasize this miserable figure the survey added that only 4% of executive director posts (including chief executive officer) were filled by women. Overall, women held 4% of directorships. There are areas, specifically in the public sector, where this figure is mocked. Compare the 73% of women managers in health and social services with only 6% in production. I leave readers to decide whether the bias against women is a hangover from centuries of traditional thinking; whether it is both this and a distrust of women in high positions in what many men consider is 'their world'; or whether a hatred of self-confident women still exists in many boardrooms, even, woundingly, among some of the few women who actually sit in them.

This book addresses these questions and many others entirely from the woman's angle. I make no apologies for this – it is a tiny correcting of the balance that has always existed – but I have avoided whingeing and complaining, and not just because it will be thrown back in our faces. Simply, I hate it. We must look at this prejudice with the clear-eyed intelligence of women who have risen or are rising to positions of huge responsibility and have succeeded in the cauldron of competitive business. It was a privilege to talk to all of the cast who were so kind as to provide their thoughts and experiences. They are all very busy women but were happy to engage in endeavours to try to warm the climate towards women in business. May I introduce them, in alphabetical order.

- **Dawn Airey** – currently chief executive of the British Sky Network, she comes from a questing background, and fought the woman's corner in her days on the ITV scheduling group. She is sporty and dynamic.
- **Sly Bailey** – chief executive of the biggest newspaper group in the land, Trinity Mirror, she began work as a telephone sales rep, and found her ambition to run the company. At IPC, she oversaw what was the country's biggest management buyout and then sold the company. She is truly an inspiration and a wonderful lady.
- **Karen Blackett** – born of West Indian parents who demanded high standards, she is the young marketing director of Mediacom and also a kick boxer. Not a woman to fool with at work or play.
- **Tina Blake** – in her early forties and from Birmingham, she has twice sold companies, one in corporate videos and the other in training. Her father's love of adventure has rubbed off on her.
- **Martha Lane Fox** – in her early thirties, she comes from an academic family and was the face of lastminute.com, which she co-founded. It boomed, nearly bust and is now making a small profit. She shocked the business world recently by quitting to take on new challenges.
- **Jacqueline Gold** – in her early forties, and another high achiever, who only began to see her potential once she was in work, at Ann Summers, where she is now chief executive. She has set all manner

of trends and has learned to fight the establishment. Bright and beautiful; a good operator in all ways.

- **Kate Hartigan** – managing director of a big German-owned bearings manufacturer in the West Midlands, she also chose to miss university when she left school. Mild-mannered, inclusive and meticulous.
- **Ricky Rudell** – began her latest business after she was 50. She started in selling and taught herself how to be highly successful by methods that are both painstaking and clever. She now owns a sandwich-making business.
- **Emma Savage** – in her late twenties, having worked on the shop floor of her father's vehicle components factory in the Black Country since she left school at 16. She now runs and owns it, battling to keep it alive.
- **Dame Marjorie Scardino** – American-born chief executive of the Pearsons conglomerate, which owns the *Financial Times*, among many interests. She is acknowledged as one of the world's most powerful businesswomen.
- **Alma Thomas** – a performance psychologist who travels the world helping international stars. She provides numerous insights into what women have to do if they wish to achieve in business.
- **Dianne Thompson** – is the effervescent chief executive of lottery company Camelot, winner of a well-publicized battle with Sir Richard Branson. She is also a mother who gave up lecturing in marketing and actually did it – in a big way.
- **Anne Wood** – mother figure to the creation of the Teletubbies and a host of children's television favourites, she set up her business at nearly 50 because she had to, and is perhaps the accidental archetype of this book.

The idea to write this book came when I was searching the bookshelves for inspirational material for women with ambitions, to pass on to a member of my own staff. Sadly, I found none.

In compiling and writing this book, I have been helped by a number of people and my thanks go to Leon Hickman, who after discussing the idea with me agreed to help me turn it into reality. His hard work in transforming my interviews and thoughts into a book shine through and I could not have done it without him. I would like to thank Jo Collins for transcribing all the tapes into copy, but above all my thanks go to all the ladies who are in this book, who gave me such great inspiration, which I am so happy to be passing onto you.

Karren Brady

1

starting out

If you want to be successful, you have to take chances. You can take them armed and prepared to meet most eventualities, but you still have to take them.

When I first visited Birmingham City's ground, St Andrew's, as a prospective managing director ten years ago, I found professional football's equivalent of a rubbish tip. It was so bad that some areas of the ground had been condemned and closed down for safety reasons. To comply with the health and safety legislation, the inspectors must have been wearing climbing boots for the crumbling concrete terraces. The offices were a warren with emphatically coloured walls, some favouring blue, as they would at a club long nicknamed The Blues, which showed they didn't have much imagination in those days either.

The manager sat in a small office on the first floor of a temporary building that stood in a corner of the ground, behind which was a railway line and a view of the city across an industrial wasteland. The players' dressing rooms were a credit to the Vauxhall Conference but, as we were in Division One at the time, nothing to boast about. Curiously, there was a theatre in the railway-end stand, proving perhaps that the players on the pitch weren't the only comics at the club. Ancient, dusty curtains hung limp and askew across the stage, and chairs stood, some of them broken-backed, in sad piles, waiting for the bingo to restart years after it had been abandoned. The pitch, I was told, drained well – better than the lavatories, I hoped – and the floodlighting worked. At least, two-thirds of it did, one-third of the lights having been removed on a previous chairman's orders as an economy measure. I then learned that the average crowd was about 6000 per match.

I wanted to take it on! First of all, though, I had to persuade David Sullivan to buy it, so that I could bring along the proverbial dustpan and brush. Oh, yes, and the disinfectant.

'I can honestly say that, even as a 23-year-old, or maybe just because I had no idea of what the problems might be, I had no fear.'

Trusting your instincts

Taking a chance? I was taking a chance with my whole career because I could see a different prospect emerging. I may not have put it quite this way on that chill February day in Small Heath when David's property manager and I stepped into my future, but I was making a business decision. Unbidden by anything but instinct, I wanted to be managing director of a football club, and not because I was in love with football – I wasn't – but I had this notion that I could be a success as head of an organization in a business not so much dominated by men as monopolized by them.

I can honestly say that, even as a 23-year-old, or maybe just because I had no idea of what the problems might be, I had no fear. I believed that, because I am self-confident and prepared to do what I feel is right no matter what the personal cost, I would do an excellent job. There would be prices to pay, I knew that, and later would discover that only by going to bed at eight o'clock could I manage to juggle a young family and a never-complete job. But I have never regretted the decision. Never once have I felt that I made a mistake in persuading David Sullivan that he should part with millions of pounds to buy the club. To be

successful you must, above all else, be able to sell – either your abilities
or your products.

> *'To be successful you must, above all else, be able to sell – either*
> *your abilities or your products.'*

David Sullivan was 60/40 against buying into this dilapidated home of
wishful thinking. Even *Keep Right on to the End of the Road* – the World
War I marching song that had echoed around the old place for 40 or
so years of Saturdays – was the fans' anthem to patience and fortitude
rather than achievement. Because he is a brilliant businessman, he could
see the potential, but he didn't acquire his reputation by backing losers
and, while Birmingham City were not quite typical losers, they were
certainly non-winners. In a hundred years of existence, they hadn't won
a trophy of more than second-class repute, and disillusionment was a
cancer among supporters, who had certainly earned the right to hold
back on their season-ticket money. But no one makes a penny by being
negative. I had done my sums and, even in a notoriously unpredictable
business like football, it was clear that even a moderately decent team
would draw five-figure crowds to St Andrew's – all the more so if the
viewing conditions went beyond primitive into the unheard-of realms
of comfortable.

> *'... no one makes a penny by being negative.'*

You may be able to smooth talk your way to a sale once, but if the
quality is bad you can forget selling it again. Maybe this is not entirely
true of football but, even in this game, product loyalty can be strained.
How else do you explain Manchester United compared with Birmingham City? So it was obvious that we had to start with improving the team
and then improving the surroundings. If I could convince David Sullivan
that my plans had a realistic chance of working without costing him too
much more than the acquisition sum, then his desire to own a football
club would do the rest. The club was never a plaything or a hobby; it had
to be business-led without soft options. He is a multi-millionaire because
he has never veered from this view – and neither have I.

Setting out your stall

The real problem was that no one at St Andrew's had a grasp of the figures. There were debts all over the place. One player 'owned' a spot in the corner of our club shop where he thought he had the right to sell his own brands. The chief scout was also the catering manager. Invoices were thrown around like confetti so that money could be drawn swiftly for various and often unspecified purposes. I'm not saying there was actual cheating but how could anyone tell if there had been? The previous owners had run out of money with the collapse of their bank and they kept laughably inscrutable records of incomings and outgoings. Indeed, within a week of our takeover, the city council demanded £100,000 that they had previously lent to the club to keep it in existence.

The place was being run without an objective. The employees were without focus and, because there was no credible leadership, there was no direction. The only thing that appeared to matter was where the team was in the league, and the answer to that was not very high at all. I had been closely involved in running a newspaper and, whatever people may think about the *Daily Sport* and its content, it was an expertly run business in a niche market. I sold the idea of Birmingham City to David Sullivan simply by convincing him that this was a great opportunity to use our business techniques in football. We would also be starting at such a low point that we could hardly help but go upwards. That was naïve perhaps. On the other hand, the arguments worked and, after three days of financial haggling, the club was ours.

He had bought the club from the administrators, taking a risk over its potential debts. Each day the bailiffs turned up and, as he had predicted, it became clear that the club was a 'black hole for money'. It was equally clear that my job was to close that hole, lay a foundation on which a business structure could be based and, in the meantime, start doing some proper housekeeping and sort out the mess. The team was losing, morale was low and all the additional revenue streams were suffering – from programme sales to hospitality, from sponsorships to kit sales. Basically, the plan had been to do nothing more than survive from day to day and hope something would turn up. Well, we had, but I have no time for mere survival – I wanted Birmingham City FC to thrive, and the only way for it to do so was by sound business techniques.

Initial change was swift because I believe that a new broom must be seen to be sweeping. Employees had to know I was strong and would not flinch from difficult decisions. There would be no unfairness if I could help it, but on the other hand business in a hurry has no time for democratic niceties. Decisions had to be reached and, with the trust of the board, I was the one-woman committee.

> *'Employees had to know I was strong and would not flinch from difficult decisions.'*

Some decisions are structural and may take many years. In my case it took over nine for the club to win promotion to the Premier League, my goal from the outset. Other decisions are cosmetic and, just as a newspaper takeover is often followed by a new look, so it would be at St Andrew's. Within a week, we had a new football strip for the players, much to the liking of fans who, only hours after the announcement of the buyout, were complaining that the Kop hated the style of the current strip and wanted to revert to one that was more traditional. So here was a way to instant popularity. May I say at this point that it did not last forever and is always patchy, in direct proportion to how well the team is doing or the price of admission. But I wasn't trying to poll high on *Big Brother*, and no one who runs a business can hope to. My job was not to win a popularity contest, but to make Blues a club to be proud of. We just have to stick to the big picture, the one that involves profit and loss, productivity, turno-ver, quality, relationships with staff and public, and, in sport, position in the league table. To do otherwise can, and does, land clubs in administra-tion and even liquidation. But for the moment I was looking at a segment of the picture. We signed two new players and tackled an anomaly that was costing us tens of thousands of pounds at the turnstiles.

> *'My job was not to win a popularity contest, but to make Blues a club to be proud of.'*

Did I fail to mention, on top of other problems, the absence of our own training quarters? And then there was the fact that every one of our terrace fans had to have a membership card, earned by good behaviour and the promise of future good behaviour. Previous management had thought the card was a satisfactory way of tackling a bunch of grubby youths who had attached themselves to our name and called themselves supporters. One such mob had proclaimed themselves 'The Zulus' and their aim was, crudely, to cause mayhem among rival fans and never mind who got in the way.

The problem was that the membership system was choking the financial life out of the club. The attendance had been fixed at the maximum number of fans in the scheme, eliminating the huge 'passing trade' (those supporters who decide to just go along on the day). The one thing I knew for sure was that a Blues supporter was not going to wake up and support Aston Villa. On the other hand, he was not necessarily able to wake up on a Saturday morning and travel to St Andrew's on impulse. He would always say he was a supporter, but how was he manifesting that support? He wasn't buying a programme, a shirt or, most importantly, a ticket, because the membership scheme made it hard for him to do that.

So the scheme had to be scrapped immediately, and it was. There were other and better ways of beating this particular demon and it would be done by creating pride in the club and what it stood for, not by restrictive measures that marked us as lepers. The aim was to build on the existing and develop the new. I had plans for a family scheme and community club, and a bunch of Zulus did not fit into that plan.

'It is vital to be self-confident and to push towards conclusions without becoming sidetracked.'

I am a logical person by instinct. I tackle subjects one by one, go into detail, reach my conclusions and move on to the next. Single-mindedness works in business and, in harness with hard work, moves mountains of paper – and dodges quite a lot of it too. It is vital to be self-confident and to push towards conclusions without becoming sidetracked.

I had to shut the player's stall in the club shop, whether or not he uttered threats to leave, and the chief scout's reign as caterer lasted only a couple of days. No doubt they didn't like it, or me, but these decisions were rational. Our food certainly improved. Only sadists enjoy sacking people but, as I was told when I was 18, it's not the people you sack who make your life a misery, it's the ones you fail to sack when you should have. My first sacking came when I was 20 – the man, probably twice my age, worked in the *Daily Sport* office in Manchester. It had to be done and I knew, as advertising manager, that I had to do it because he was my responsibility. I believe that one of the biggest mistakes you can make in business is to keep on the people who continue to fail to contribute. The one sure outcome will be that your business will go bankrupt. I much prefer to employ people smarter than I am – it shows, I like to think, that I am smarter than they are.

Young people are generally positive and I like to employ them, especially if they have the A1 ingredient: enthusiasm. There is nothing more endearing than eager people, ready – now – to try anything. There may sometimes be a slight reluctance by women to put themselves forward, although this is vanishing with the changes in our culture. In all the professions, women have proved to be just as logical as men – in my experience, even more so. They have plenty of stamina and are much more loyal. All of which is why I set about employing more of them at St Andrew's.

> *'The way to please in business is not by pussyfooting around difficult areas, but by delivering.'*

Defining your approach

Anyone setting up a business finds the early days the toughest, and certainly the busiest, supplemented by a mere three or four hours of sleep. There will be days when you wished you had never embarked on the project, especially if there are banks in the background. It often helps to have a confidant, perhaps a former boss or relative with whom you can mull over the whole scene. In my case, I talked a lot with David Sullivan and his advice was usually precise and accurate. Sometimes, though, decisions have to be made on the spot based on your judgment of staff and the prevailing circumstances. I like clear and concise negotiation and if sometimes there is a bit of temper involved, then a handshake.

I was a pioneer as a woman in the upper reaches of football club management and at first men often treated me with exaggerated courtesy. My experience is that this state of unarmed combat does not last long. Most men learn quite quickly that condescension is not the quickest way to a businesswoman's heart, or anywhere else. The way to please in business is not by pussyfooting around difficult areas, but by delivering. This is particularly true of football, where the things that happened yesterday are prehistory. Dial your mobile phone to check facts, by all means, but be wary of employing it for second opinions, especially during in-office negotiations when its use smacks of under-confidence. Remember: you are in charge.

'My business success has been based on a philosophy that, instead of thinking about where we are, we should concentrate on thinking about where we want to be.'

During that chaotically enjoyable time of self-generated upheaval I learned different things about myself and my abilities. The reality struck me even then, though, that success is acquired by constant perseverance and damned hard work. At St Andrew's it was a case of not getting bogged down in current problems but concentrating on where we wanted to be, and that really meant developing a much more professional business base. It is true that every business has its peculiarities, but in this respect football has more, far more.

To begin with, it's a madhouse. In what other area are more than 90% of businesses in the red and still continuing to function? In what other area do the employees draw at least 60% of turnover and in one or two instances even more than 100%? Where else does public scrutiny go far beyond the annual accounts right into the life and habits of staff? Most men who crash cars, leave the wife or go to the pub twice a week remain happily anonymous. In football they are headlines. In the Premier League, they are big, black poster headlines. It is not my job to manage these men, or at least all but one of them – my husband! But in the end the club is answerable for everything around it; too much so, in my view.

In this respect, as managing director, I tend to be the one called on to defend or explain. I can certainly say this: success is not developed in ease and quiet. Only by thought, determination and hard work can goals be reached and ambitions turned into reality. My business success has been based on a philosophy that, instead of thinking about where we are, we should concentrate on thinking about where we want to be. I had to find out what was wrong with my business before my competitors profited, then I had to establish our priorities and go to work.

Being successful in football has always been equated with the team's position in the table or how well it has been doing in the cup. This is still true for the great majority in the Football League but the truth comes with a rider for perhaps a dozen clubs in the independently run Premier League: those clubs to whom this status and all that goes with it – £15m from television rights for a start – is all-important. For them, success starts to be measured from fourth from bottom of the table, which means avoiding relegation and the sudden ice water of comparable poverty that comes with it.

Birmingham is one of these clubs and, although supporters may not wish to hear it, it has to be run on sound financial lines. While it would be ridiculous to describe players who cost £5m and are paid £1.5m a year as second best, we do have to buy from a pool marginally below star level – where star level is a £15m signing-on fee plus £4m a year in wages! Backed by millions of supporters, Manchester United is a worldwide industry and able to afford hugely expensive players. Chelsea is a Russian billionaire's chosen one, but United is a far more applicable model. The management have learned that they should operate to firm business structures because the money required to buy a team can be self-generated.

In our business, like any other, we have to ensure that we walk that fine line between risk and reward – it's just that the fine line is but a thread of cotton. This means we must be scrupulously careful when we buy and contract players. Every player purchase is a risk and, moreover, one that we can't hide from prying eyes. A bad buy is to be seen by thousands tripping over the ball twice a week. It is one of the problems of dealing with human beings rather than nuts and bolts. I have learned one lesson above all others in the past ten-plus years and it is that I know very little about football so I leave the choosing of players to the manager. More than this, after working with variously good and average managers, Steve Bruce, our current manager, has proved to me beyond doubt that the manager is the most important person at a professional football club.

We have learned that we should operate to firm business structures because the money required to buy a team can be self-generated. If you spend all your resources on buying the team and not running the business, you end up falling from grace – like Mark Goldberg at Crystal Palace. In general terms, don't dream – work. Don't over-extend – plan. Make sure you know where you wish to go, and push. And if you use a few feminine wiles, don't go around thinking it's unfair that you should have to. Exult in your power to move things along the path you chose, and don't be deflected.

So where and how did I reach the point at which I could begin to draw these conclusions?

'The truth is that ability is what you are capable of, motivation determines what you do and attitude determines how well you do it.'

I have always been a hard worker. I used to help my Nan do her cleaning job when I was ten, getting up at 5.00 a.m. during the summer holidays to go to work with her, not because I had to but because I wanted to be involved in doing useful things. I enjoy work, and still do. My principle is that nothing is work, unless you would rather be doing something else. I have always been enthusiastic about what I do, and made sure that, whatever task I was given, I did it to the best of my ability while trying to keep a smile on my face.

I have found from the various places that I have worked and the environments I have been in, as an employee and as a manager, that the world is full of willing people; some willing to work and the rest willing to let them. I am not academic, something that nagged at me for years until I realized that this did not make me any worse, nor those with a list of university degrees any better. The truth is that ability is what you are capable of, motivation determines what you do and attitude determines how well you do it. If I had to select one personal characteristic I regard as being key to my own success I would pick determination.

On the road to achievement are all manner of temporary defeats – even failures. When you suffer a defeat, the easiest thing is to quit, or not try again. That's exactly what the majority of people do, but this book, as much as anything, is about women who haven't given up. Women who have objectives and meet them. Women who keep right on learning and working until, often much to their surprise, whole new vistas of business opportunity open up. I hope that some readers will be inspired by their example, and become the movers and shakers of the future. To adapt the saying, just pick yourself up, put on your favourite Versace frock and do it all over again!

Getting on with it

At 23, I was told to make Birmingham City FC work. I made mistakes, I know that. My temper was occasionally as short as my skirts. I knew I had to be flamboyant and that I was personally identified strongly as the club's Ms Fix-It, moving Blues into the new millennium. Certainly I found the media side unexpectedly complicated, but my purpose in life was, and still is, Blues and only Blues.

I realized early on that a lot of people have a misconception about what football is. Just as, say, arranging a timetable for Parcelforce is more complicated than merely ordering up a van, so football is substantially more than about turning up on Saturday, picking the team and winning the game. The team matters above all else except, of course, winning. Winning is the ultimate, but getting the parcel there is more than a game: for me, it has to be the mission, the serious side that is my contribution to the joy – let me gloat here – when 50,000 cheered our team to victory in the 2002 play-offs to get us promoted to the Premier League for the first time.

This was one of the best days of my life, when all our dreams where turned into reality. All the hard work and long hours justified. Proof that nearly ten years of transforming a derelict club was worth every blessed minute. And then, a few months later, 30,000 cheered our team to victory over Villa in the first league match against our local rivals since 1986. Could being an addict to achievement get much better than this?

Soon, however, this was to become an example of a high point with a dramatic downside. The club was fined for a small pitch invasion that, regrettably, also included a spectator assaulting the opposition goalkeeper. I felt aggrieved. Time has taught me that it is profitless to dwell on a perceived injustice and, briefly, I burned with exasperation. However, women have an inbuilt ability to swallow the bitter pill and get on with life, and with the job. Machismo is a male concept.

Yes, football is a game, but it is also serious, if not – as some of its blinkered adherents regard it – more important than life itself. These days it also has to be a business, and the business side of it is marketing, catering, hospitality, commercial sales, ticket sales and customer development. Then there are retail, the media and the Internet. Ten years ago at St Andrew's, everything bar selling tickets was either in its infancy or did not exist. Richer supporters took executive boxes as a favour to the club. Probably half of them were empty and a number of others were on short-term leases. The catering was strictly pork pie and sausage rolls, and hospitality meant bottles of spirits in the boardroom.

We had to draw up plans for each area, bringing in fresh faces and ideas. We talked to supporters, businesses we dealt with, other clubs. We consulted staff at regular meetings and in time introduced initiatives, many of them breaking new ground. Building new stands was a priority but we had to fill them and to do so we started a number of schemes. 'Kids for a Quid', a scheme to allow under-16s to come to games for £1, was instantly successful and has been widely copied in various ways in the entertainment industry. Competitors forecast that we would come a cropper, but we chose our matches carefully and watched, fascinated, as our fan base among children grew and grew. We knew we had a reputation problem and we knew that some of the most calming influences in life are women and children, so how were we going to get more women and children into the club? We created a family stand.

How were we going to get back the fans who professed to love us but preferred to stay away? We were going to get their kids and make it cheap for them. We didn't want free admittance because if you give something away people don't really value it. Our theory was to make it cheap enough for them to come and then still cheap enough, but a little dearer, for them to return. The key was to get them to come the following week for £5 and then £10 and then become season ticket holders. That was the plan and it was successful.

Fan loyalty in football is such that your first club is your last, and we introduced plans that a lot of clubs weren't doing then and aren't doing now. Every week you have 30,000 people in the stadium and you should advertise to them: leaflets on the turnstile; advertisements, information and marketing over the tannoy and in the programme. You can't miss an opportunity to sell what you have to sell. We built for the future and in our first season in the Premier League every St Andrew's Blues seat was filled for every match. We also embarked on a series of promotions and started to advertise in newspapers, magazines and on local radio stations. As a matter of fact, we still do – one of the few clubs in the country to pay for media coverage. I tell my staff that we have at least 23 events a year and our job is to ensure that each one is a sell-out. Once the game is over, the opportunity to earn from it has gone forever. Never knowingly miss an opportunity to sell. That's business.

> *'Aspiring, ambitious people don't exit the field when the blows start coming.'*

As I said earlier, football is a black hole for money. Once the hole had been identified and marked with 'Danger' signs, we had to generate cash. Simultaneously, I had to try to be a bit of an accountant, a marketer, a motivator, a disciplinarian and a visionary. Mould these areas together and it is possible to create a unique blend. Nevertheless, the key point to all this is hard work – to have ideas, to encourage other people to have ideas, and to see them through. This may sound as simple as a click of the fingers. Take my word for it, or that of anyone building a legitimate business: it isn't. It is blood, sweat and fears. No tears? I'm not the crying sort.

Making a difference

Building your own business, though, is rewarding, exhilarating even, and, strangely enough, making money to buy a fine lifestyle is nowhere near the best of it. The absolute essence, the drug of doing it yourself, is in creating an infant concern and then organizing and running it until it is a healthy money-maker. It has to be mothered through all manner of crises and I have to say I am surprised and disappointed that there are not more women at the helm in football.

Change in a small business can usually be taken at a gradual pace. There are instances in larger, ailing firms where it has to be forced, and forced fast. Force was necessary at Birmingham City. People were kidding themselves that eventually everything would work out, that life in a rut was actually quite pleasant. I had taken on the job of being a force for change and, while we tried to temper hard decisions, it wasn't always easy. People were moved along, contracts ended. Each problem had to be dealt with separately. There were times when I cursed Birmingham and could have walked out. No way. Aspiring, ambitious people don't exit the field when the blows start coming. I was young and a woman in football, the kingdom of the male, but I knew I could tackle at least as hard as most blokes I had seen making their way up the business. To succeed in business at the moment, women have to have balls: more balls than most men. And there has to be a vision, one that you know you can fulfil, as I have at Birmingham, by whatever means necessary.

So in that first year we set about doing the things that were necessary to win promotion to the Premier League. We hadn't a minute to waste our energies on the niceties of life; we had to be focused and dedicated and if we made a few enemies it was for the good of the club, the supporters and the city. We had to hold the celebrations, though. Within a year of the buyout we were relegated to Division Two and lost our manager. So what did I do? There is a great temptation at times like these to sit around and count your bits of bad luck, your failings, your poor decisions, your orders that were misinterpreted or ignored – in other words, a good old wallow. Never do it. Be more positive than ever and show your face everywhere with a cheerful look on it, no matter how you feel. Tell yourself: 'This is never going to happen to me again.' And don't let it. Optimism works wonders and I know because it was a long journey back to the top division.

Women also have wonderful powers of endurance. In 1997, with the invaluable help of Roger Bannister, my financial director, and within a year of having my first child, Sophia, I floated Birmingham City FC as a plc on the Alternative Investment Market. It was an exhilarating time, full of self-discovery, but immensely hard because, well, I wanted to be with my baby. So when I wasn't chasing from Birmingham to London or working to near-exhaustion, I was in my set-aside time with Sophia. The flotation was probably my greatest personal achievement, especially as at the same time I became the youngest MD of a plc in the country. It also showed that for the first time in its hundred-year history the club was on a strong financial and structured footing: the job I had been appointed to do.

It was a do-it-ourselves affair, really. We used outside resources when required – our solicitors, SJ Berwin, and our stockbrokers in particular – but generally we did the work ourselves, making presentations all over the country to sell the shares and saving a good deal of money, possibly as much as £1m, by doing so. It was a means to an end and raised £7.5m – money that was to enable us to rebuild the railway stand, and increase capacity.

It was a massive learning experience for me. Being a plc focused our minds on how we should run and operate a company. It made us act more professionally because we have more shareholders and I am responsible to all of them. Some entrepreneurs consider it a noose around the neck but I quite like it because it is a form of control on illogical dealings. It certainly allowed us to enlarge our business. And I am sure that Sophia is having a wonderful childhood.

The greatest achievement for the club was winning promotion to the Premier League and I played my part in that by ensuring that it could acquire the right players at what we regard as the right price. We don't chase success at the cost of all else, and never will. In football there is a secret balancing act to be identified by each club, depending on whether they are Manchester United, Yeovil Town or Birmingham City, and I like to think that we know when pressure can be applied to one end of the see-saw or the other.

There are clear differences between football and ordinary, sane, business but knowing when and how much to push, or when to pull in, is common to all of us if there is to be a profitable future. Our pushes and pulls are clearer than most because football clubs are under closer scrutiny than any other business in the world. Every utterance, every transfer, every decision is followed with anorak intensity. How many businesses have reporters devoted entirely to following every twist? When we make a mistake – and we have made a few – supporters rage publicly, even to the extent of chanting your name in hatred. Yes, I have heard it several times. Frankly, you would not want it to happen to a dog. And when we have success? The delirious noises are aimed at the manager and players. And I would never expect cries of 'We're in the black, we're in the black' to stand a chance of replacing *Keep Right on to the End of the Road*. But our fans do appreciate the way the board of directors has led the club. I know this from the response we receive in letters, faxes, telephone calls and e-mails. I would like to thank them all, and to add that, for me, the incentive is not the applause of the crowd but the creation of a hugely successful business.

Key lessons

- *Do your sums before getting involved in a new project. Also, do your market research and know how much 'support' you can draw on from your customers/clients.*
- *Be confident. Back your own instincts with decisive action.*
- *Have clear goals in mind. What exactly is it you want to achieve? Know what your priorities are.*
- *If there are long-term problems with stop-gap solutions, look for alternative ways of tackling the issue.*
- *If possible, find yourself a mentor or confidant. We all need advice or just a sounding board now and again. But remember, you are in charge.*
- *Be creative, if you can, in finding new ways of generating cash for your business.*
- *Be prepared to take knock-backs in your stride. It's all part of the experience.*

the ten principles of success

The half-serious joke is: you don't have to be Superwoman to achieve great things in business, but it helps. Well, it would. However, the fact is that none of us is. My belief is that the successful ones have two or three areas in which they excel. In others, they will vary from very good to average. In my case, I am no financial expert. I don't read the *Financial Times* every day, and I find reading balance sheets considerably less interesting, although far more revealing than *Hello!* magazine. On the other hand, I have a foxhound's nose for scenting a deal, and her patience in pursuing one.

I understand instinctively whether I am going to be on the winning or losing side in a deal, an instinct that has been educated by negotiations in the football transfer market. I also know that I have to make as much as possible for the club on the business and commercial side and then leave practically all other financial matters to accountants. Similarly, although I am a football enthusiast, my knowledge would not extend to naming England's 1966 World Cup winning team in full. Birmingham City football is the manager's affair. The single characteristic to be found in every successful businessman or woman is determination. So that is the quality that tops my list.

1   Determination

When I started work, I was the first one in, last one out. Sickness? Didn't do that. To this day, I regard sick days as for other people. I tried to miss holidays as being a waste of time. When all my friends were putting on coats to leave work at 5.00 p.m. on Fridays, I was tidying up and helping to do what needed to be done before the weekend. I always asked other people: 'Can I help you with that?' I used to read the company brochures and if we were supporting a charity I'd ask if there was something I could do; I would be delighted to join in.

I wanted people to know that I was more interested in my business – advertising – than I was in anything else, and I was determined to show people who I was and what I could do. It took nine years at St Andrew's to win promotion to the Premier League and of course I have been offered other jobs, some of them most attractive. All along, though, I have remained wedded to the notion that I have to succeed here.

'I was determined to show people who I was and what I could do.'

This tenacity was certainly called upon when I had the task of manipulating a way for Steve Bruce to take over as manager of the club, even when he didn't know that that was what he wanted to be. Steve had made his name with Manchester United and ended his playing career at Birmingham, where he impressed all the directors with his common sense and maturity. He was our target and my job was to pursue him until we had his signature. First, as I implied, he said publicly he was staying with chairman Simon Jordan and Crystal Palace. A week later he changed his mind. Simon refused us permission to approach Steve and it was then that I had to ask myself how far I was prepared to go to secure him.

There was the potential for a court case and a heavy penalty by way of compensation. It was then that I went back to my formula question:

what is the worst that can happen? Had we been threatened with, say, losing 20 points, we would have withdrawn, but it appeared that the worst that could be done to us was to have to pay substantial compensation. We went ahead. We were taken to the High Court and Steve was told he would have to wait a month before he could join us. By then, though, I think Simon had assessed his position and seen that he would be unable to keep Steve, no matter what he did. We paid compensation and, because this is an odd world, Simon appointed the manager we had sacked, Trevor Francis. The club had been trying for nine years to reach the Premier League, five of them with Trevor, and Steve did it in six months.

2   Ambition

Without at least an element of ambition, you are not really a starter in anything bar falling asleep out of boredom. I realize that when they are young, people don't exactly know where they are aiming, or perhaps I should say, don't know where they are being carried to. Sly Bailey, Anne Wood and myself are examples, but there is a point when you realize that you are good at something and then, because you are good at this thing and you are confident about it, ambition begins to form. I am not talking about a Richard Branson type of ambition, the type that awakens the apprentice tycoon at 6.00 a.m. and he decides he wants to rule the world. It is more like falling into the job: first, knowing you like it; second, knowing you are good at it; and, third, knowing other people think you are good at it. Next thing you are thinking: 'How can I go further doing this thing I like to do?' Or it might be someone who is struck by an idea, as Jacqueline Gold was. She reckoned that parties for groups of women would be a slick way of selling more Ann Summers items, and she was ambitious enough to go out and organize them in their hundreds.

So I think ambition is important, but it is not necessarily formal ambition, like wanting to be a barrister or doctor. So, no, I never thought when I was six that I wanted to be MD of Birmingham City, but when I saw an advertisement in a newspaper offering a football club for sale, suddenly I knew that running it was something I could do and wanted to do.

As I mentioned, St Andrew's was falling down and the club was desperately short of investment. Building a profitable business from such impoverishment appealed to me enormously. Don't ask me why, but by some mysterious process I understood that Birmingham City would be the challenge of a lifetime, one to which I could devote all my energy – not because it was football, though, but because it was potentially an exciting business waiting to happen in a big city. That is my kind of ambition and, when it came to it, I did persuade David Sullivan to buy the club. It wasn't that rare thing that a very few people have, of wanting to claw their way to the top regardless – it wasn't as naked as that – but there was never any doubt that I was going to strive to reach the top and, once in the Premier League, to sit on various committees and to be part of the establishment of football, which I now am. And that ambition has carried me into other areas: journalism, authorship, chairing the new West Midlands radio station, *Kerrang!*, and I'm on the board of Mothercare too. And, yes, I am still very ambitious.

3   Confidence

There is a fascinating interbreeding between ambition and confidence. As you grow into a job, you realize you are good at it and then you might suddenly think: 'Hang on a minute, I am better than him or her, so why am I not up there?' You have the confidence to want to try other roads. Making decisions increases your confidence, although I must say that in business terms the confidence to choose the right option consistently is possibly an attribute you either have or don't have. As Alma Thomas says elsewhere in this book, there are ways of building your confidence, but I believe that there are people who can't, or at least don't wish to, make decisions that can have important repercussions – and women especially are afflicted with this condition.

Confidence is not an ingredient you can touch; it is a mental process and comes from realizing that you have a talent and from reaching sound conclusions, based on knowledge, preparation and understanding. Understand your business and you should have the confidence to make decisions. My area of under-confidence comes from not having had a university education. There are a number of us in this book who didn't go to university, and we tend to think that at some point someone is going to tap us on the shoulder and say: 'Hang on a minute, you haven't got a business degree. What are you doing here?' It has been a concern for me that I haven't been as polished as the next person. But then I take an objective look at myself and I think: 'What are my worries? I floated my company in 1997, I became the youngest MD of a plc in the country, I sit on the board of Mothercare, I'm the chairman of *Kerrang!*, I go around the country speaking about my business success, so why am I not confident about my background?' I think it is perfectly acceptable not having been to university. In some ways it makes you sharper, more competitive, especially in an instance like mine, where I have a sales and marketing background.

4   Courage

Courage stems from confidence but stands alone as a tremendous asset. Setting up your own business demands the confidence to believe that you are capable of running it, often alone, and to do so if you are mother to young children is in the area of gold-medal courage. I meet many women who have given up a good job, sold the car and mortgaged the house in order to back a business idea they believe in.

> '*Courage stems from confidence but stands alone as a tremendous asset.*'

This can be a huge risk and sometimes it doesn't work out. The bravest of the brave will have done this several times before they succeed. Such people discover the loneliness of the small-time businesswoman, a condition that is isolating because the person is not in the positive surroundings of an office where she is a team player and can hide a little behind other people. Suddenly all the hours under the sun are her hours and if she doesn't put them in, she risks a business failure.

I must be honest and admit that I guess I lack courage in this respect as I have never gone it alone, as I have always worked for someone else. Most women almost drift into owning a business. They have a job on the side that develops until it takes up more time, and probably pays better than employment. Then they switch, but, unlike men who devote their entire working energies to their operation, some women remain responsible for other concerns in life – their family, the cooking and housekeeping, looking after aged parents, that kind of thing. That is what I mean about courage. There are several illustrations of it further on in this book.

5 Humour and charm

These are such important qualities in a woman that maybe placing them fifth in the list is too low. Suitably used, they will become an indispensable part of your public personality; indispensable, too, in negotiations and trying moments. By charm and humour I mean anything but flirting or wearing low-cut tops or short skirts, any or all of which can be juvenile, off-putting and counter-productive. In a male-dominated business environment I have found the use of genuine female charm to be devastatingly effective. Men like welcoming smiles, calm and friendly discussion together with a dash of the cool analysis that they often find surprising in a woman, although I have no idea why.

Charm is locking in with the personalities of other people, making them think they are extremely important to you, listening carefully and remembering their foibles and concerns. Oh, yes – and smiling at their jokes, when they are appropriate. Abroad – in the Far East for instance, where women are expected to be two steps back – charm and confidence knocks men sideways. People are more willing to work with those they like and who respect them – people who smile when you first see them. When I was growing up in business you never saw the chairman. He was unapproachable and, as depicted in films, 80 years old, very serious and very unconnected. He is the person you don't ever want to be. You should actually be most approachable and you should remember that it is far more productive if each staff member enjoys work as much as possible. Not every setback is a crisis and sometimes you have to pick up the pieces and laugh at what has happened.

Perhaps the male equivalent of charm is charisma. Whatever it is, it has helped me make a lot of better deals than I would have done by trying to be tough. People like someone who remembers that little

Johnny has been ill or who tries to cheer up a girl whose boyfriend has left her. Football is highly competitive on the field, sometimes even viciously so, but I think a rival who knows that a club has had some kind of problem and drops a note to a chairman or MD wishing it well will always be respected, even when at some time in the future there is conflict. Little things are key to good relationships. There is a world of difference between being a drunken yob trying to be one of the lads and being a professional, charming woman: a woman of whom it will be said that she is helpful and interested and not pretending to be something she isn't. I don't like women trying to be males, set on breaking a competitor's balls. People, both customers and rivals, enjoy the experience of being charmed. Seeds sown in that way are extremely potent. After all, it is much easier to be charmed into a decision than to be blasted into it.

> *'It is easy to become bogged down by too many hours and too many burdens, and laughing things off, sometimes laughing at yourself, really does work.'*

Laughter is a miracle medicine and at times being able to laugh at yourself and your struggles puts them in lighter relief. This may not be the full cure but it certainly eases liverishness. It is easy to become bogged down by too many hours and too many burdens, and laughing things off, sometimes laughing at yourself, really does work. I am able to say to myself: 'God, I am a prat, I can't believe what I have just said.' Barry Fry, a manager at St Andrew's, is famous for his zany behaviour and daft humour and there were times when I just had to laugh at him or with him, otherwise I think I would have torn my hair out. On one occasion I was so uptight that I stormed into the dressing room to drag him out of the shower. Goodness knows what I was thinking about but we were soon giggling about it. We still do. Some jokes do remove tension but merely cracking them is no antidote to hard times where, as the terraces song has it, 'always looking on the bright side of life' and trying to stay positive at all times definitely does work. You have to realize that everyone makes mistakes and says odd things. Remaining in good humour is always more effective than dwelling on them.

Here's a very good example. One of our directors, a lawyer, happened also to be acting for George Best's wife, Alex, and when he turned up at her house during an estrangement there were dozens of photographers outside. They asked him who he was and he replied he was from the *Jewish Chronicle* and in he went. Two minutes later, the doorbell rang and when he asked who it was a voice said: 'I'm from the *Jewish Chronicle*.' It was pure Monty Python. I was laughing at this story so much that it became infectious and the whole restaurant was laughing at us laughing. In the end, the manager came up to us and said: 'Madam, Miss Brady, you are in the Dorchester now', as if it were a sin. That started us off again.

Football is a strange and unusual business in that, as I said, clubs are competitive on the pitch but not often in the various markets outside it; or maybe only a little, for a decent share of televised matches or for sponsorship. Every so often there are problems over transfers or contracts or, in one case, my criticism in a newspaper of West Ham. The unwritten rule is not to take such things personally because, frankly, you wouldn't have a friend left if you did.

At St Andrew's we tend to use humour to disguise or ease conflict. We had a long dispute with Wimbledon over a player and there were fractious moments. However, we kept the wires open between the clubs and although the dispute ended in Wimbledon's favour we never totally fell out with each other. You can guess that Simon Jordan wasn't too impressed over losing Steve Bruce but I pointed out to him that in football: 'You will go into the arena and so will we: nothing personal. We will both do the best we can for our respective companies but we should respect each other as professionals and not actually fall out. There will come a time when you might want a favour from me because actually the world of football is very small.'

6   Leadership

Martin Luther King famously said that the ultimate measure of a man is not where he stands in moments of comfort but where he stands in times of challenge. Those words are so important to me because they define the meaning of leadership; it's not always about how much you know what to do, but how you behave when you don't know what to do. On the brink, under immense pressure, how you can respond, how you react to people and how you can show people the way truly determines the amount of leadership quality you have.

When we decided we wished to appoint Steve Bruce, many supporters were thinking 'why Steve Bruce?', because his managerial record defined him as someone who did not stay long at a club. But it was time to lead. So it was when we decided to float the company and, possibly most of all, when the team was relegated. I bet if a child took over at Old Trafford for one match the chances are that Manchester United would win, but it would take genuine leadership ability to run, say, Exeter, and lead them back to Division Three. I see the full package in Steve Bruce as a leader and motivator because, largely, that is what football management is about.

But how do you break down his skills? He is respected by his players, but why is he respected? He is liked, but why? He is humorous at the right time, but how does he know the right time? He is a confidant to players, but why do they trust him? He is tough, he is straightforward and he is respected by players, supporters and the football world in general. He has made his early managerial record look like the blip it was. It all adds up, I think, to Steve as the boss communicating to people in under-standable language what he is trying to achieve.

A leader must also be visible because people, increasingly, are failing to respond to someone purely because he or she has a title. Obviously it helps to have the authority inferred by a title but the initial impact fades should the leadership be low-grade. Shareholders and, to a lesser degree, employees are demanding a bigger say in the way their company is being run. Their first priorities must be that whoever has their trust is qualified to do what they say they can do, and that this person communicates fully and honestly with them. They then want their leaders to have vision and the confidence to tell them where the company is and where it is planned for it to go in the future, whether that is one year's time or five. They should also be shown the steps the company is taking to reach a recognizable point, because ultimately people want to invest or to work in a successful, well-respected company. They worry about constantly checking over their shoulder and wondering if at any minute they are going to get the sack or the company is going into administration.

I think that as a leader it is also important to be self-aware – to know where your skills are and to know your weaknesses. I am very aware of holes in my knowledge – in particular, as I mentioned earlier, a lack of comprehension of some of the finer details of tax law and suchlike. Clearly, it is necessary that someone on hand should know these things, and I have never had the slightest hesitation in calling in an expert. There is always trouble around the corner when people tackle financial matters without quite knowing what they are doing – so I recommend that if you have doubts, as I do, spend the money and hire someone with expertise. No shareholder, colleague or employee is going to respect you if you try to dogpaddle through the financial maelstrom. They must have absolute confidence in your decisions and the basis on which you make them. Which brings me back to communication.

7   Communication

This is such an important principle, and one that is often honoured more in the breach. In larger organizations, letting people know what is happening is too often left to three or four newsletters a year, a few notices on the notice boards, and word of mouth. It has also been my experience that managements fail to trust their staff with facts before significant change is to be made, or let them know too late to be able to do much about it. I call that *fait accompli* management.

Normally, the last people to know what is going on in a company are those who work there. It is not sensible to let confidential information out of the boardroom, or to give plausibility to rumours by denying them. On the other hand, management have to assume that their staff are reasonably intelligent and prefer to know the detail rather than allowing barrack-room lawyers full range. I prefer to err on the side of knowledge, against ignorance.

'The most motivating tool possessed by a manager is letting staff know what a vital contribution each member makes.'

Generally, women are far more genuinely communicative than men – I am not talking about gossip here – and are capable of putting over difficult decisions with empathy. Women talk to people and care what they think. Men love to be triumphant and are less happy with anything that indicates they might not be perfect. I am always surprised by the interest our staff show in how and why the club makes certain decisions. I honestly believe that if at 3.00 a.m. I were to ring up any of the people who work for me and tell them we needed them in the office immediately, they would trust my judgment. It doesn't matter if you work at Manchester United or in a meat-packing factory, you have a right to know whether your company is being well run. A major reason why people leave is that they think management is incompetent and they haven't a chance of being heard. They think no one understands their point of view or even cares that they might have one. The most motivating tool possessed by a manager is letting staff know what a vital contribution each member makes.

There is a subject closely related to communication and it needs to be addressed because it strikes to the heart of the failure of many women to fulfil themselves in business. It seems to me that modern women divide into two categories. There are those who fall in with other people's standards, and in today's society this usually means they become 'one of the lads' who regularly go boozing in the pub. I am sure this was the genesis of the ladette culture.

Then there is the second category, those who are made nervous by their position, lack the self-assurance to continue to mix freely in the office, and become unapproachable. These executives are victims of what I call the Queen Bee syndrome, and they consistently cause damage to the prospects of other women with ability. They refuse to encourage talent and don't like to see able women promoted, on the theory that 'I've made it to the top and I don't want to be challenged by others.' They introduce obstacles to aspiring women along the way and are inclined to team up with male chauvinists to criticize them. I have seen a good deal of this and I find it very strange indeed.

Why should it be that there are so many Queen Bees in human relations departments? And why is it that a woman head-hunter often sets different, and higher, standards for other women? It is my experience that this is so and I have very capable friends and acquaintances who believe that women in positions of responsibility can be a woman's worst nightmare.

You may assume that the women bosses who appear in this book are not of this type, although, goodness knows, all of them have strong char-acters. I have also tried to avoid the stereotypical idea of women bosses – those who wear shoulder pads and shout at people a lot because they don't know any other way. They are almost more macho than the male bosses. All my examples of successful businesswomen are by their nature givers, nurturers and creators. Far more so than men, women believe in serving their company to the best of their ability. They are unbendingly loyal to the business, constantly willing to direct their ambition solely toward the interests of the company. They are above promoting their best friend or being ultra-political in the boardroom. They will actually sit down and say: 'What is the best thing that this company needs to do at this stage?' – as Sly Bailey did when she sold herself out of the top job at IPC. She could have tried to hold on to it but she believed she knew what was best for the shareholders of IPC, and sold it to AOL Time Warner.

8   Staying on track

Becoming distracted endangers positive thinking and making progress. In sports businesses, staying on track is the equivalent of keeping your eye on the ball, concentrating on the objectives you set yourself. Fail to stay on track and I'm afraid you will be run over. This advice extends to whether you are running your own business or climbing upwards in a company. The fact is that you must learn to refuse because if you don't you will find yourself in all manner of compromising situations.

Later in this book, two young businesswomen talk of how boyfriends tried to pressurize them into doing less work, and there are, I know, thousands of instances of women being pulled off course by other attractions: spending too much time on hobbies, on projects that have nothing to do with work, on jobs within the office that are never going to be productive, and even – and this is a controversial area – on family affairs. Being able to say no is a significant sign of maturity and of single-mindedness. The noes extend to invitations to parties. A long weekend?

Serve on this charity committee? Cook his dinner? These might or might not be sacrifices, but it is a certainty that you will have to make some, and probably even more, should you be working and trying to set up your own business at the same time. This takes a lot of self-motivation, but what a challenge! And what rewards you can gain in terms of self-worth, self-assurance and self-sufficiency. There are occasions when it is vital that you plan your time and ration it.

In a slightly different context, you can also waste a lot of time and energy on being over-careful not to step on someone's toes. Be diplomatic, of course, but don't dodge issues just because someone might be touchy. There are only so many hours in a day and moving sideways is not the best way to use them. In work, I see a lot of people who have 20 reasonable ideas and then try to juggle them. It is much better to focus on the best one you have rather than spread yourself too thinly. Make the idea as simple as possible and stay firmly with it, too, rather than switching to another at the slightest setback.

When you discover a business you really enjoy and ambition begins to dawn, decide objectively on the next step and think about who in that department can help you and how you can bond with them. Good people will get a kick out of guiding you and will be flattered by your interest, at least they will if they recognize you have a talent for the job. You will make friends and find mentors in this way.

Incidentally, you will soon learn to ignore jealous people. Think logically about the future. Football usually defies logic, although there are certain criteria. At the start of a season, supporters oozing optimism declare that the team is good enough to be promoted. Very positive of them, but for the club such ideas are a complete distraction. We look at it this way: if our team is going to be promoted, we have to be in the top half of the league by Christmas, in the top three by March and top in May. Those are realizable targets if you have a squad of outstanding players. If you don't – if you are Birmingham in their first (or even second) season in the Premier League – the simple aim will be to stay as far away from relegation as possible. To do that, as we did, we had to make our financial assessments, so we bought six new players during the time we were allowed to, at the start of the new year. I have to say, neither the manager nor the board ever veered from this survival formula.

I have found that working mothers develop two personalities: simply, the work personality and the home personality. The trick is to keep them entirely separate and in balance, so that one of them doesn't outweigh the other. Probably from the time Eve served Adam, women have been capable of doing more than one job at a time, and I am sure this stems from having children and satisfying their needs. These days the jobs are likely to include cooking, ironing, shopping, housework, to none of which a woman can devote her whole attention. Often she lives in organized chaos. The sight of a mother racing round a supermarket, pushing a trolley and steering her children away from trouble, is commonplace. Quite possibly she has already done a day's work at the office, returned to pick up the children, start the washing machine and dash out again. And then there may be that nag of guilt that she should be at home all the while, and maybe questions from her friends about why she should be so ambitious.

Managing the balance of these two separate lives has to be achieved by trial and error. I feel quite confident that I have it because my children are happy and healthy. My family know that I love my job and I wouldn't be the same person if I wasn't doing it. Each working mother has to find her own formula though, because what is right for one of us will not be right for someone else. Increasingly the balance in marriages and partnerships has been achieved by the man acting as a house-husband. However, many women don't wish to see their partner in this role, no matter how much it helps them cope. Nannies and childminders may have parts to play, as may close relatives. My mother and my mother-in-law were invaluable in helping me after I had my babies. In the end, the solution has to be your own.

9 Giving it a go

At one stage or another, everyone in business is frightened of failure. It paralyzes some people, particularly a certain kind of woman, while it energizes others. Be driven, because an opportunity missed through fear or timidity should be far more frustrating than an attempt that fails. Those people who keep trying will eventually succeed.

Not everyone who has had an idea has been successful, and many have failed only to see someone else make it work. I am thinking here of the inspiring courage of James Dyson and his revolution with the vacuum cleaners. He asked himself: 'Why should a vacuum cleaner need a bag?' and invented his bagless 'dual cyclone' machine. He was ridiculed, and when the ridicule stopped he faced lawsuits and imitators but he refused to be diverted from manufacturing and selling his vacuum cleaner to the world. Had he backed down, I have no doubt that another manufacturer would have taken up the system and made a fortune.

There is also an impression that setting up a business is an all-or-nothing exercise, whereas in fact there are often a number of methods of securing advice or financial support. The Internet is a marvel for finding help and, indeed, I would recommend a short tutorial course on IT for anyone ignorant of how to use it and about to start a business. There are government schemes in most towns and cities, and the cost is often minimal. Banks are frequently helpful and a visit to an accountant is also worthwhile, particularly one knowledgeable about sources of grants and loans. If you wish to borrow money, always compare at least three banks, and do the same with accountants and lawyers. Never forget, either, to ask for quotes from three different companies on all equipment and furniture. Saving on items like these can make the difference between profit and loss. It is amazing how cheaply things may be bought if you look around. Equally, it is a mistake to provide services and not charge for them, unless it is a fair exchange. There are many roads to Carey Street and the bankruptcy court. I can guarantee that two of the quickest are giving when you should be charging, and poor billing of customers.

Certain risks are not worth taking. In particular, don't go rushing into a business before you have checked the market for whichever goods or services you are selling. If you are prepared to remain employed and to work on an idea from your home, turn one room into a study and build up the business to a point where you feel comfortable. Birmingham City plc chairman, David Sullivan – one of the richest men in the country – carried on in his job in an advertising agency, and only when he was making more a week in his own business than he was earning at the agency did he decide to leave to do it full time. Basically, you are asking yourself whether you can afford to devote your entire week to building a business, and part of the assessment has to be paying the costs of setting up and of initial services. So make calculations before you take risks, but don't be afraid to take them.

10 Hard work

Some pundits would say that it is not about the hours you put in, it is about what you put into the hours. This is partly true but also illusory. When you are in business or seeking high office you have to accept that you put in genuine time, and a lot of it, as opposed perhaps to hiding behind a screen at the back of the room. I have found that, in the end, hard work resolves everything I have ever been asked to do. Sometimes the hours are enormously productive and sometimes they are a grind. If you haven't put them in, however, you will never discover just how high you can go.

Key lessons

- *Use the ten principles of success as your guide to achieving your dreams.*
- *Know your strengths and weaknesses – if you need to improve on your areas of weakness in order to fulfil your plans, work at them!*
- *Remember to use all the characteristic advantages naturally available to you – and exploit them to the full.*

3

making your mark

After interviewing many of the country's most successful women, I began to ponder on what they had in common. They all stressed how hard they worked, but that did not come as a surprise: fourteen hours a day was about the average, dashing from meeting to meeting, checking make-up, clothes, hurrying down a lunchtime sandwich or healthy salad as they read e-mails or accounts. No doubt businessmen work similar hours, without the make-up checks. I then listed:

- determination;
- breaking down barriers, including male prejudice, although this was not necessarily strong on everyone's agenda;
- open attitudes, firmly on the female side of the balance, this;
- willingness to take risks, even enjoyment in taking risks, an element missing from many women, I feel;
- pleasure in the power to make a difference;
- creativity;
- belief in new ideas.

Overall, the list was long.

In the end, one skill stood out in them all; one indeed to which the male employees of women always seem to return. They agree that, unlike many men, senior women executives are able to switch from area to area seamlessly, moving from one subject to another and back again with barely a moment's hesitation. You might say that this is the product of thousands of years of practising homemaking, and possibly it is. As a tool in business it can be dazzling, and in negotiation as powerful a weapon as any caveman's club. Not always as powerful as a quiet deal in a gentlemen's club, but that is an operations area from which – thank goodness, I say – we are barred.

Standing out from the crowd

Women are rarely as clubbable or conspiratorial as men, and this might be seen as a drawback. But to be far more positive, one man, a financial director, both of whose seniors are women, produced this remarkable tribute: 'Women are far, far better to work with. They are more inclusive and are able to work on a number of levels at the same time. I wouldn't swap them for a male regime at any time.'

Alma Thomas, from her experience as a performance psychologist in great demand by celebrities and business executives in the US and Britain, holds trenchant views on why women can be excellent in business:

'I rate those women who do succeed in business very highly. I suppose people will think I'm bound to say this, but I believe it implicitly. They have special skills, sometimes different from men's, but that does not make them less effective. In fact, I have found they are most efficient and one of their key strengths is how supportively they manage people.

'It is said that men think more logically than women, that men have one direction and go for it. We tend to get bound up in extraneous issues or side-issues. There may be something in this but it often means that women have a scope that men don't. Anyway, many women are very capable of the logic that makes them achievers.

'Because women are poorly represented in some executive areas, particularly in business, there is talk of positive discrimination. I don't subscribe to that at all, not at all. It is down to women to get hold of what they are trying to do, do it and be damned by all the doubters. Now I have to stress here that it takes a lot of guts to be focused and remain focused no matter what perceived failures may come along the way. But who the hell cares about failures?

'The problem can be, as I said before, that women take on so many roles that they become deflected. It's not easy to be wife, mother, cook, housekeeper and remain on the ball, and sometimes women who are successful are seen to be very difficult and aggressive. The assertive way isn't deemed female. Things are changing a little. We see women in rugby and football now. That's fine. What appals me is that many young women today just ape men's behaviour in drinking and that kind of thing. It's okay if they wish to drink but surely they should have enough confidence to establish their own rituals.

'Women don't need men to lean on – they can do it by themselves. However, many seem to think they don't need to, don't feel they can or can't be bothered. They don't want to give up other things to branch out in their own areas, and it's true you have to give up many things to be able to concentrate on your ambitions. There are no shortcuts, you just have to and that's the end of it.

'My daughter has just started a business and she's saying she's always knackered and there's no social life. It certainly isn't a cosy life and it can be very difficult indeed. Sometimes I am beside myself I have so much to do and so little time and I wonder why I'm not like everyone else. Well, it is very hard work but it's wonderful; I can't tell you how wonderful and exciting. When it comes down to it, women who are passionate about success have to be different. They have to think differently. It is rare when they say: "I can't do so-and-so." They are the people who say: "Yes, I can." Then they go home, all done in.'

There are a number of inspiring stories in this book. I have conducted interviews with women who impressed me, including:

- Anne Wood, of Ragdoll, was motherly and kept telling me that she was just an ordinary woman who knew nothing about business. I am not at all sure about this: she seemed very cute in surviving several minor crises and cashing in on the legendary success of *The Teletubbies*.
- Martha Lane Fox saw the evolving and exciting possibilities of the Internet and lastminute.com was founded.
- Jacqueline Gold wanted to change the philosophy and culture of the sex industry, and the result was Ann Summers.
- Dame Marjorie Scardino, chief executive of Pearsons and several times selected as the most powerful businesswoman in the world, believes her achievements are founded on lessons she discovered from the financial failure of a small-town newspaper.
- Dianne Thompson, the dynamic chief executive of Camelot, the lottery company, has a history of reviving weary causes. She once described herself as 'a woman with balls – balls of steel' and my suspicion is that all women high-achievers have to be ferrous from head to toe.

There were few common traits among these women, although one caught me by surprise. A number, including me, had been to schools that were founded for boys and remained predominantly populated by them. It would be my guess that prospering in a boy's world, in what one headmaster I know used to call 'the underworld of boys', steeped us in the half-anarchy, half-comradeship that passes for growing up among the lads. We have no fear of the full-grown version, no matter what his current guise. Behind the exteriors that may now be sophisticated, brash or bullying, there is the boy who we called 'swot', or 'cocky', betrayed by acne or bad breath. And we recognize quickly whether we are in the presence of a tiger, a fox or a rabbit. If anything, we prefer men's company, but only when it doesn't involve clothes, cosmetics or shopping. Martha Lane Fox, casually brilliant, put it this way:

'I do realize I am very fortunate compared with 99.9% of the rest of the women in the population. I had an incredible education at a school in Westminster and then at Oxford, I have had the luxury of a family who have never said: "Go and be conventional," and I

*can honestly say my mother would have fallen off her chair if I had
said I wanted to be an accountant. She was so much happier when
I said: "I don't really know what I want to do but I want to change
the world."*

    *'And I know that those are things that have helped me in business.
It wasn't a set pattern. I think all I can say is that, thanks to the luxury
of my upbringing, I am where I am. Other people have never had
the privilege of my background.'*

The roots of success

Dawn Airey was also in a small minority of girls at a boys' public school.
I am not sure how much she would support my theory about the extent
to which this background helped her to succeed, in her case to become
MD of the Sky Television network. However, read this and I think you will
agree that it might have, albeit not in an inspirational way:

    *'I wanted to be a veterinary surgeon and the masters at school said:
"You won't get an A in physics, Airey, so forget it." What the masters
tell you at an early age, you sort of believe. I thought: "That is fine.
If I can't be a vet, what am I really interested in?" I was very angry
and I was going through my socialist phase at the time. I'd have the
Socialist Workers Party news-sheet delivered every week and when
there were mock elections at school I would stand on communist
and socialist slates, which went down like a cup of cold sick. But
again I didn't care, as that was what I believed in. I think if you don't
go through a left-wing phase in your teens or early twenties there is
something wrong with your psyche!*

    *'When I was told I wouldn't get into veterinary college, I turned
to the next thing I was interested in, which was telling stories. I was
always interested in news and current affairs, so it seemed sensible to
be an analyst or a producer, so that is what I fixed my mind on – and I
didn't change. Ironically, I never got to be a producer in current affairs.
I didn't get to be a journalist, although I did work on some regional
programmes in my days at Central Television in Birmingham.*

'So I did my A-levels and I hated school with such passion I was traumatized by the experience. Some of the masters I just did not get on with. I was just too much of a free spirit. I remember the first day I was at school, when there were only half a dozen girls and we got to meet the monitors. These were the "gods" who were allowed to wear brown suede shoes and white shirts. They could also walk across the grassy knoll on the way to the chapel; so I get to meet this guy, sort of sitting there preening himself. He was called Damian McKenny and he said: "I am Head of School."

'So I said: "You are number one creep, then?" and there was this stunned silence among all these other monitors behind him. It went all the way around school: "Someone has called Damian a creep."

'It went downhill from there really, but again I said what I thought and I suppose I didn't have a relationship with those people. The girls who got on best had relationships with the right monitors and the right heads of school. It was a touch of Lord of the Flies, and I was just bored. My parents had not taught me to fit into structures, they just said: "Go off and be yourself, be true to yourself and say what you think, be inquiring, do not fit into predetermined roles. You are not a predetermined peg to fit into a predetermined hole."

'I went into this boys' public school and it was all about that. It was all about rules, regulations and adherence to the code, whereas I pushed all the time and it didn't go down desperately well. The school do contact me now and ask me for things.'

Anne Wood made an astute point when she said that it was better for girls to go to a boys' school and for boys to go to a boys' school, too. Wood, who introduced Roland Rat to an unsuspecting world, went to a mixed grammar school and was brought up in a North-East working class family during and after World War II. Not many girls went to university in those days and even fewer were entrusted with business, even if many of them efficiently propped them up as secretaries and do-it-alls. It was a shocking waste of creative ability – half of the human race excluded from areas in which I intend to show they possess just as many innate skills, even if they differ. This prejudice continues to exist, although it might have changed its form. This is what Martha Lane Fox said about it:

'I get asked a lot about why I think there are not more women at senior levels. I think women are immensely capable and add a dimension to an organization that is vital. I would feel very, very worried if the team we have built here was 90% male or 90% female. You know the world isn't like that and you need a balance to reflect it, and both parties bring equally valuable and important qualities.

'Part of the reason there are fewer women is that the structure of businesses and the way that they work has recently been dominated by rewarding that more male type of characteristic and I don't think that is a good thing. If you had a female chief executive officer, she would be more worried that her team was all-male or all-female than a man would. Men don't even think like that. I think that I am quite unusual in some of my characteristics and I don't like generalizations, but I see some woman who work with me and I feel very lucky not to be like them.

'I'll give you an instance: when men want a pay rise they come to me and say: "I want a pay rise and I want £10,000 more, please," and when women want a pay rise they say to me at the end of another meeting, or e-mail me with the message: "I am terribly sorry to ask you this, but can I possibly trouble you, I know it is probably really difficult but would you mind looking at my pay?" I always go back and say: "What do you want?" Bear in mind these are very confident women, but there is a different type of confidence that men seem to display – an arrogance about their own ability, in a way. Like: "This is what I want and I am going to get it and I am going to ask for it."

'It is partly my education, at school and at university, that again made me think in a traditionally more male way, so I can hopefully find a nice combination. I certainly don't feel I have had to become a substitute man in a man's world. I am not like that, although I am very lucky in that I have done it through my own business. It has been lastminute.com that has put me in the position where I can be me. I don't feel I have had to play a game or compromise, and that is fantastic.'

It wasn't with a hammer but with a sweet smile that Dianne Thompson broke into do-it-yourself in Britain, becoming the first MD in that business when she was appointed by Sandvik of Sweden. She said:

'I was also their first senior manager and this really was the turning point of my career because until then, as a woman, I felt I had to prove myself more. When I was at ICI in the '70s they did actually say to me at the interview that to be treated equally I had to be at least 10% better than the men.

'In my early career I had this feeling that I had to prove I was good, and when I arrived at Sandvik it was interesting because everyone's attitude changed. Staff seemed to think: "God, she must be good as she has got the MD's job." It was the first time I didn't have to prove myself. I hope I did, of course, but I didn't have to because people assumed I must have been good.'

Jacqueline Gold comes from a background which is just as exotic, if entirely different. Her father, David, was one of the founders of the sex industry that began to surface as a legitimate, multi-million pound business in the 1960s. It was entirely dominated by men and the needs of men until Jackie and one or two other women robustly intervened and began to transform it from under-the-counter in grubby, blank-windowed shops to in-your-own-home among the girls.

Shaking the tree

Today, as chairman of Ann Summers, she can boast of a £110m turnover and 7500 employees as well as twice winning court battles against entrenched institutions. Logically, Jackie knew from the day she began to revolutionize her father's business 20 years ago that she was the equal of the men she dealt with. Over the past two decades, there have been huge breaches in masculine sovereignty over the arts and professions but, in practice and certainly in the commercial arena, her experiences continue to be relevant. She said:

'The transition was interesting. I found myself compensating for my sexuality, thinking that because I wasn't a man it was some kind of weakness, and because I wasn't older [she was about 20] I didn't fit the stereotypical picture of a business person. I would go in for elaborate hairstyles, I would wear severe business suits – unusual for me because I love feminine dress – and there I was, all severe, and in glasses as well.

'It wasn't until I did an interview on GMTV and somebody commented that I looked like a politician that I began to think seriously: "What am I doing? To whom are you trying to prove something? What does it matter?" It was a turning point for me because I thought: "Be yourself, be how you want to be," and the hair came down, I dressed how I wanted to and I relaxed. Instead of worrying about the way I came across and the way I looked, I concentrated on what I knew.

'My advice to anybody would be that if you know what you are talking about and you know your business or career, as long as you know your stuff, that is the greatest power of all. Neither have I ever been one of those women who emulate men in their business style. A lot of women think that they have to be aggressive to be successful. I have my own style and I am a good listener. I am quietly spoken and I like to listen first before I contribute, and after one particular meeting where men were in a big majority, one of them came up to me afterwards and said: "I actually find your quietness quite unnerving." It is easy to underestimate the subtle approach – you don't have to smack the table with your hand; you can be confident and quietly spoken without being aggressive. But I stress that you have to know what you are talking about, and I don't ramble as some people do.'

Dame Marjorie appears to have risen effortlessly to the top ranks after the Georgia experience. She is almost matter-of-fact about her elevation – I imagine Frank Sinatra would have called her 'a cool dame'. This is her opinion of how she practically fell upwards:

'I had no plans. I thought I would be a politician because I am from Texas but I had always been involved in journalism and then I went to law school. During law school there was the Vietnam war and the invasion of Cambodia, all of which happened before you were born. My law school closed for the semester and I found a job working for Associated Press. I went to West Virginia and met my husband and we decided we would go to journalism school and it all evolved that way.

'I finished law school so that I could make money so that we could start a newspaper, and that's what we did. It was our joint ambition at that point, so I practised law and I worked at the paper and he edited the paper in a pretty small town in Georgia. The newspaper won a prize but it was an economic disaster, a total failure and of course I was in charge of the business side so I learned a lot. That was a turning point, because when you learn, you notice that if you try something and fail, you don't die, and nothing ever really scares you that much again. You know you can carry on. My husband went to work for the New York Times and I went to work for The Economist, where I eventually became president.'

My own father wondered who might give me a job and then concluded that I would make rather a good estate agent. No doubt he recognized an early ability to sell and, in my own way, to organize. I suspect that he was being paternal rather than condescending, but I had no intention of becoming an estate agent. I'm not saying that there is anything wrong with starting your own estate agents and then buying and selling property. Someone I know has done exactly that, buying a regional section of an established practice and employing new ideas, fresh marketing techniques and graphics. But I had grasped a different perspective and, love him as I do, I did explain to my father in a few short words that the idea had no appeal to me and that I would take my A-levels and ambitions elsewhere. No doubt about one thing: being surrounded by all those boys had given me independence of mind.

Finding your niche

From the age of 18, I had a variety of jobs and made some impact as I was always able to sell. I have to admit that I am not a very sociable person; I quite like my own company and thoughts and most nights I was in bed early and at the weekends I would close the door to my flat and not do a lot, except watch television and generally mooch around. I was by no means a recluse but I found that work, and particularly being in charge of a business, provided me with goals. The inspiration was doing tangible work, changing things by my own efforts. Making money was important but self-respect and self-reliance, moving business along, were far more so. Others found this to be true too, none more so than Sly Bailey, chief executive of Trinity Mirror, who began work in telesales on a national newspaper and overnight uncovered an identity as a top businesswoman.

As the daughter of David Gold, an early entrepreneur in his industry, Jacqueline Gold was at an advantage compared with most young women but, as her parents split up when she was 12, with her father leaving home, hers was not a business environment. Indeed, as a lively teenage girl, there were many other things to do and she neglected her schooling, preferring to find opportunities to work. At 13 she quickly demonstrated her need for financial independence by designing crossword puzzles, for which she was paid £50 a time. Her father gave her a job at Ann Summers and then:

'At first, all children are shy in the adult world and I was 21, so very young, when I began in this business. I also looked a lot younger than that and I was going into what was perceived then as the sex industry, a business completely dominated by men. I wanted to go in and change the whole philosophy and culture, moving it from the sex industry to an acceptable business that was very appealing to women. Not only was that a difficult challenge, but you can imagine the type of comments I came across on the way. I couldn't even go into a restaurant without the waiter making a remark about a banana or something ridiculous like that – but all of those preconceived attitudes, I am pleased to say, are now very much in the past.

'I had always wanted to run my own business but, like most people, you almost fall into what you want to do by accident. I was actually working in the wages department at Ann Summers, in a sort of interim role, but I wanted to do something more creative. I came across two women who at that time were having selling "parties" in homes and they asked me if I would like to go to one. It was then that I got the idea of doing Ann Summers parties. Don't forget that at the time it was a very male-dominated business and when I took my idea – a very female concept – to the all-male board, they were sceptical at first. After all, I had no business experience as such and I knew practically nothing about the direct selling industry, which is what I was proposing they should enter. I was actually forced to rely on feedback from those people at the party.

'Anyway, the board tentatively accepted the idea and I started with eight organizers. I have 7500 now, but what I saw as a disadvantage at the time – not having the training or experience – I would say now, without a shadow of a doubt, has turned out to be a strength. I had been thinking freshly without any previous baggage, and that was vital. There aren't enough companies who are prepared to gamble on this kind of initiative.

'Being a good listener is more of a female trait, I think. I remember doing a speech at a direct selling conference, because our success was evident and we were growing so rapidly. Of course, all the MDs and owners were men. Several came up to me afterwards and I got all sorts of comments, including "Did you write that speech yourself?"

'The comment that I found most incredible was from the MD of Jasper Cosmetics, which, maybe not surprisingly, is no longer in business. He said: "Do you really have women on your board?" I said: "Yes, we do." He said: "Well, why?" I replied that we were running a company whose goods were essentially for women, so obviously women were going to have a much better understanding of women. He was running a cosmetics company for women and he *didn't have one woman amongst their executives. I think that says a lot really.'*

It has often been said to me that women are not business-inclined, in the sense that they are seldom self-driven in a quest to run a firm or factory. By instinct, they do not like to take the risks that are often necessary. Their comfort zone is around nest-making. I am sure there are grains of truth in all this. Perhaps through aeons of conditioning there is a genetic state of preferring love to war, or prettiness to power. This is by no means all bad. No doubt, one day it may be explained. However, the manifestation of this in commerce, it is further claimed, is that somewhere in the story there has been a man to lean on. He might have been dad, either by the legacy of a company or by handing over power. Or he could be a husband or boyfriend with whom our female entrepreneur has formed a partnership. My initial reaction is that women include the man because they are too kind to exclude him. However, some confirmation of the 'man's shoulder to lean on' view appears to be provided in those lists of the 100 Richest Women, starting with the Queen, whose treasures were largely acquired by the male line. No more than half a dozen will have risen to this 100 from ordinary suburbia, and several of these will be pop stars. Anyway, we are moving on. I have one perfect example, not high-profile but highly representative of women brimming with ideas who are captivated by business building.

Tina Blake sold a Birmingham corporate video company and, with her husband, has created a mini-conglomerate centred on organizing short-course training for a variety of big companies, managing conferences and speech training. Her upbringing appears to have similarities with Martha Lane Fox's, in that, while it was eccentric to say the least, in business matters it made her independent, driven and self-confident. She left one company because the owner refused to make her a shareholder and then set up her own on the principle that she had an essential core staff but employed freelances to film the videos under her direction. Having sold that company, she set up another, Aims, again as much as a facilitator as an actual producer.

Her childhood had been a riot of action. The story of the obstacles, including slight dyslexia, that she cleared on the way to setting up her own business should be an inspiration to those thousands of secretaries who believe, not without a good deal of evidence, that they could do the job better than the boss. Typical of so many women in business, she runs an ultra-tight ship.

'My father, who is a doctor, was a huge influence on my childhood. When I was six he chucked me in the River Severn and told me to swim. There I was in my little green two-piece bathing suit and sud-denly I was in the water. Of course, I had learned to swim by then and it wasn't dangerous, but it was the kind of thing he did with my brother and me. We started skiing when we were very young, at about four. Mum would be there with hot chocolate when we finished and, anyway, we'd spend most of our time in the skiing hut doing colouring books and being made a fuss of.

'One day – I think I was ten – he took both of us to the top of quite a difficult piste and skied off, leaving us to find our own way down. I thought: "Oh, my God!" but at that age you just do it and no doubt he was nearby somewhere, keeping a check on us. I think that was the same holiday my brother broke his leg. Looking back, all the out-door things we did made me pretty impervious to physical risk.'

There was in Tina a tomboy element and, like many of the successful women in this book, she had a wonderful childhood, full of adventure. She went to a public school in Birmingham and then to Millfield in the sixth form because she wanted to be a television researcher and a mini-studio had been built for pupils there. Edgbaston High was no prepa-ration for Millfield, however, and attitudes she found there came as a terrible shock. Indeed, they were reminiscent of Dawn Airey's. A further coincidence was that Dawn, like Tina, was rejected by the BBC. They learned early on that there was no such thing as failure.

'My education had been very ladylike. I was pretty intelligent and good at sports. I suppose I was a leader, but I had no aggression, so that when I joined the sixth form with only a few other girls, I felt very

unpopular and I have to say I had never been that before. On my first day there, one girl came up to me and said: "I don't like you." It taught me that not all people are nice.

'I had always wanted to work for the BBC and I went for an interview before deciding which university I should go to. My parents wanted Oxbridge but I favoured Westfield College, London, because they did a media course there. My mind was made up at a BBC interview, where the woman who recruited trainees told me it didn't matter whether or not I went to Oxbridge. Throughout my time at Westfield I just assumed I would join the BBC. When I went back to make my claim, the same woman told me: "The BBC only recruits Oxbridge graduates, my dear." I was thunderstruck.

'Mum had died by then, father had remarried and I went back to live at home. My father persuaded me to go to a secretarial college, where in six months I had 100 words a minute shorthand and advanced typing. Afterwards, I temped and even worked for the Duran Duran fan club, until opening packages with teddy bears and sweaty knickers in them proved too much – in three weeks.

'Briefly, I became a secretary at Harrison Cowley, an advertising agency, and convinced myself I was the equal of anyone there. I used to rewrite their press releases but they never gave me credit and I became fed up, so I advertised myself in the local newspapers as "Lively and intelligent graduate who would like to work in marketing, video and TV." I had a number of replies, one of which was from David Clement who had recently started Optical Image, doing corporate videos.'

She became his Girl Friday. He was a technical wizard but preferred not to be too involved on the business side, which was how Tina uncovered her talent for running a very tight ship and making a sound profit. Furthermore, he was a stickler for high standards and that, too, suited her.

'Our joke was that he was never happier than with a screwdriver in his hand because he had been a carpenter and built the whole studio, furniture included. We were a very good team because he taught me the technical side while he left me in charge of the whole marketing strategy. He believed in the highest possible standards and that was a terrific lesson for me. It did not matter if we took three weeks on a video; it had to be the best – a priceless asset as it happened, because there were loads of cowboys in the business at the time.

'He mortgaged his house to buy all the latest kit and he must have had the utmost faith in me because he left me to do the budgets. Our customers liked him enormously, he was a marvellous figure-head. He would promise the earth and then try to deliver it, even at a loss. Yes, I was soon in charge of the budgets. In those days, the mid-1980s, corporate videos were a big thing and although I was only in my twenties I was dealing with MDs and senior managers. There was a bit of the "Hey, little girl" but it made no impression on me. Now even Joe Bloggs thinks he can produce a good video, and it isn't like that at all.'

Tina was head-hunted by a satellite television company at this time, but was not sufficiently involved and after about two years of produc-ing things like rugby, fencing and pop concerts from a mobile unit she returned to Optical Image as a director. However, there was a business downturn at about that time and she found herself becalmed. David Clement had turned the company into a facilities unit because there was little corporate video work and she admits that she sat tight, doing things like marketing, until 1993 when she quit because he wouldn't let her have any shares.

'My plan was to MD a small company producing educational videos for grant maintained schools but there was a snag and I was soon on my own. I was lucky that a video offer came in at the time and David let me use his studio, which was most kind. Really, it had been a weakness of mine to think I needed a partner. The reason was that I had only £3000 in the bank and I am not a business gambler. I was forced to take the risk and it worked.

'It seems to me it is a common thing among women that they aren't prepared to risk capital. I mean I've taken all sorts of risks to get business but not with finance. I didn't buy my own equipment,

I rented it and made less profit because I might have no work and not be able to continue paying for it. I'm good at managing and bringing in business. I've never had a bad payment or not been paid. Customers have to be up-front with payments and I'm not saying that's the best way, it's just the only way I can cope with. I have a feeling this attitude is pretty general with women. We are tidier by nature.'

Overcoming your fears

In case you should be worried that over-caution with cash could slow her company's advancement, the story that follows will convince you otherwise. Psychologist Alma Thomas reckons men's and women's brains are wired in different ways – thank goodness for that, I say – but adds that some women have more male genes than others, giving them a more aggressive and, I would say, perhaps a more hard-headed approach to business. How many women would be genetically predisposed to take the chances that Tina did on the non-financial side, I don't know, but certainly she had chutzpah. She explained:

'I never turn business down. I have moved into all sorts of areas because I've been daring in accepting challenges. I was asked if I could advise the Boots managing director in public speaking and I said: "Yes, of course." I was given the job. Now obviously, when you are doing videos, you often have to help people in front of the microphone, sometimes with the aid of an autocue. I've done all that, but I hadn't taught anyone how to stand up at a conference and speak to hundreds, maybe thousands of people. By that time, I was doing conferences, which came about because I was asked if I could. "Yes, of course," I had said. This wasn't strictly true. In fact, it wasn't true at all. But I knew I could do it if I had a go. I knew about most of the technical side and I could plan the rest of it. Oh, yes! Boots' MD was very happy with my advice and we moved on from autocue to speaking from notes, and he's good.

'Since then, I've done a lot more, and speaker training is quite a good part of the business. The same is true of conferences. We do them for huge numbers now, as many as 6500. It was a bit of an experience after Boots had given me their logistics conference because I hired a company who promised they had sent all the equipment and had actually sent the wrong stuff. I had made the mistake of going for the cheaper option. As Basil Fawlty used to say: "I think we've got away with it." Well, we did. It was after that conference that I was asked to coach the MD to speak and then I was given a second conference for 5000.

'The most important thing is that I surrounded myself with people who did know how to do these things. I was a bit surprised, though, when I booked an organizer with conference experience to work for me on that one, only to discover three weeks before the day that he had no more experience than I did. What could I say? He was only doing what I had and it turned out well.

'Then I was asked if I could choreograph some dancers. "Yes, of course," I said. I went to keep fit classes and organized out a routine to the hit "Chain Reaction". It was very simple but it worked. Same bloke asked me to choreograph dancers and I did that. Went to keep fit class, did it – "Chain Reaction". I did it again for another company, this time with two ballet dancers, although I have to admit they knew much more than me and were very helpful. They tumbled around like they do between programmes on BBC TV.'

After selling 2 Step for a substantial sum, Tina and her husband launched a business called Aims, which handles and franchises the training of the staff. Among clients were some of the biggest drinks companies in the world. They recently sold that business too, for a handsome six-figure sum. And, if you want an example of business acumen, she has a business plan to make a profit from her experiences after she, most unfortunately, suffered a bout of ME.

Key lessons

- *Recognize that you don't necessarily need to rely on other people to make your mark. Finding your true inspiration is the best way to make great progress.*
- *Cultivate your own personal style and people will start to take real notice.*
- *Don't be bullied into doing something you don't believe in.*

4

selling your dreams

Martha Lane Fox calls herself an 'evangelical salesperson', a definition that fits many of the women in this book. I knew, too, from the moment I met Dianne Thompson, chief executive of Camelot, that her silvery voice was so seductive that door-to-door salesmen would buy encyclopaedias from her. Martha admits she flirts with customers, and while that once might or might not have been true of Dianne, she makes the point that after she had been appointed MD of Sandvik people listened to her as if she were a sage, whereas previously she might have struggled to hold an audience.

Of all the women I interviewed, I suspect Sly Bailey is the supreme saleswoman, moving up the corporate ladder at a speed that would have been inconceivable for a woman 30 years ago. It was easier for a woman to become queen than to become a chief executive. There are various facets of selling and in the context of this book none is more central than the technique of convincing customers in all forms that they should make an investment in your particular talents. This subject is a book in itself and applies equally whether you are negotiating with banks, bosses or buyers. Impressing people with your own virtues is fundamental for any businesswoman.

The personable Dame Marjorie Scardino, chief executive of the Pearson empire, must have been especially adept at influencing people in her rise to become the world's most powerful businesswoman. To a certain degree, straight selling of goods can be taught, but there are people who by temperament find it difficult, and even embarrassing. As for closing a deal, they couldn't close a door. To those people, I would say this: don't try to be an entrepreneur. You might attack your career from another direction, in public utilities or the professions perhaps. Accountancy could be attractive to you, but if you do it, here is a small plea from me: don't, please don't, choke enterprise with columns of figures or blight it with gross caution. Government bureaucracy wastes more than enough of an executive's hours and energy as it is. There are accountants who have set up in business but they are mostly practices for more accountants.

Selling with conviction

Even before she and Brent Hoberman set up lastminute.com, when Martha was employed by Spectrum, the business planners, she was told to stand up in front of a television company and make a presentation. 'I wasn't scared of appearing in front of a crowd or a group of investors. I guess I'm a complete show-off. My attitude is: "Look you guys, this is exciting – see what we can do." I am a real evangelical salesperson. It is not an act; I really believe in what I am doing.'

You have to if you are in charge of a business. While a good seller can sell bad goods, she will not be welcome when she calls next time. But an employee selling a shoddy piece of goods doesn't have a reputation to build or protect; a business does. Football is odd in this respect because no one can ever guarantee the end product, which is winning matches. What you can provide are first-class conditions for watching and it is no accident that a huge rise in attendances over the past decade has coincided with the big improvement in stadiums. At Birmingham City, we have rebuilt the facilities, and have improved the image of the club from a dreary outfit drifting towards anonymity into a vibrant modern football club with big ambitions. We are, in short, a proper business with plenty of income streams besides pure football.

The difference between selling, say, a car and selling your own personality is acknowledged by performance psychologist Alma Thomas, who says:

'We're fine at selling those cars but in my business and in big business it's about me or it's about you – you as an up-front, get-the-job-done person. Successful women are very successful at making people notice them and at selling their own talents. Unlike men, we tend not to advertise our wares obviously. Some women will think: "Why tell everyone about myself?" The best saleswomen, though, are those with a lovely, quiet self-confidence, a sort of arrogance that isn't quite, certainly not in a despicable way.

'When I make this observation, some women see it as denigrating, but it isn't. There's nothing wrong with being good at something, knowing it, and exuding confidence. Women need that approach more than men do, I think. Women are also too aware of what they can't do and are very good at saying no. I can't be like that, and successful women are very reluctant to say no to a challenge, certainly in the early years of a career. It's also perfectly acceptable not to be good at something, realize it and then say you can't do it.'

Alma is right and many of the very successful women in this book have that 'sort of arrogance'. It's self-confidence, isn't it? Those who aspire to great things must have it. Jacqueline Gold does. She had a different selling job to do when she took her idea of sexy clothing parties for women to her board. Of this ordeal, she says:

'I was desperately nervous when I went to my first board meeting and put my ideas across. It felt like going to your bank manager and asking for a loan to start a business. I was also a little shy when I had to give orders – don't forget I was very young – and I remember once trying to hire a conference centre in Coventry and I couldn't get the men there to take me seriously. I had to dispose of that kind of image, but they were difficult times. I was driven because I felt so

passionately about my business and about what I was doing. It was this that gave me the willpower and confidence to carry on.

'Today, whether I deal with men or women, I treat them the same. If possible I like to talk face to face. Not only is it easier, there is something much more personal about human contact than the phone, fax or letter. With men, I am always very straight-talking; I never beat about the bush, and they prefer this way because they know where they stand. There is no misunderstanding of what your intentions are and you are not dragging the situation out.

'Women can be overly passionate about their business and per-haps too determined and prone to disappointment. Sometimes it is time to let go, if things are not working. I have dealt with male and female franchises and women can get much more emotion-ally involved with their projects. In Los Angeles, I remember the franchise negotiation with one woman dragged out to eternity, far longer than with any man. There was real difficulty in persuading her to the way we work and then getting her to buy into it.

'On the other hand, when I took my ideas to the board it was obvious that they had a male culture in place. They didn't seem aware that women as well as men would buy our products in huge numbers, and that they would insist on high quality and first-class service. When women go shopping they demand a lot more from the store and the retail company than men expect. I addressed this early on. We have a big quality control department and we do every-thing in our power to make sure the customer comes back. We want people to have respect for our goods and our company. There's nothing I hate more as a customer than being treated shabbily or talking to people on the phone who patently don't care about me or their employer.'

Kate Hartigan, that rarest of women, MD of an engineering company, believes that star saleswomen are born not made but – don't despair – that most of the skills can be fine-tuned into the others. Like most women, she prefers persuasion as the way to sell, while recognizing that a touch of aggression may be necessary. 'Women may not like the feeling of failing that inevitably occurs at times,' she said. 'I think the traditional roles of men and women may come into play because, whereas there will be a little voice in a man's head saying he has to provide and keep going until he succeeds, in a woman it will say: "Back-pedal, no one will think the worse of me." Only time will overcome this but the indisputable rule is that the good saleswoman gets the bigger percentages, but everyone fails at some point.'

Ricky Rudell was in her early forties when she went into business as a one-woman band, determined to sell an idea that struck her as she leafed through a duty-free magazine on a BA flight. She had been in duty-free before, mainly selling lighters, and realizing that this trade was close to being legislated out of existence in the European Union, she was looking for fresh income. It struck her as she read the magazine that a particular product for sale was foreign and that the market was wide open for an English manufacturer.

Spotting the golden opportunity

Ricky is an attractive blonde with a gentle approach to selling and she was unprepared for the attitude of the sales manager of the English manufacturer, although she is not sure whether this was because she is a woman or because he was being defensive about his job – or a mixture of the two. Anyway, when she approached this man he rudely told her: "Go away, we only supply our own shops." He was, in Ricky's words, 'negative and nasty and I wonder whether he ever discussed the idea with his directors.' She persisted, explaining how much of the market the firm was missing and how they could capitalize on their Englishness, not only on aeroplanes but in airports, on ferries and at ferry terminals, and in railway stations. A second meeting was slightly more fruitful, in that she was invited to a third meeting.

'I thought I should show them that I was a serious businesswoman who knew what she was talking about, so I took along a friend who had just made a fortune from selling his own business. I hoped he would provide a kind of gravity and a guarantee, although, as it happened, he said very little. Eventually I was told I could be their agent

with the task of selling to airlines and ferry companies. In duty-free, airlines purchase once a year and, because of this sales manager not helping, I realized I was going to miss buying times, so I went into one of their shops, bought a load of samples, put them in a suitcase and went round saying I was an agent. I knew I had to prove that the market was there and I did so.

'With the end of my previous job I had lost my office car and so I asked my husband to drive me to Monarch Airlines, one promising prospective buyer. My husband drives a Bentley and parked it, I must say, unobtrusively in their car park, but I think the Monarch people were a bit surprised when I arrived with my suitcase full of the product while a Bentley stood waiting. Their chief buyer loved it and has remained a friend ever since.

'So I got their account. I redesigned the packaging because it has to be a certain size, and, after a lot of hard work convincing them, managed to land BA, P&O, Stena and a number of others. I went back to the company in the middle of this and told them I had a list of agreements but I didn't say who they were with until they set me on as a freelance agent. I believe implicitly that everything has to be right if you are to optimize sales and so I employed merchandisers to move around the ships and ferries to make sure that our displays were there and looked attractive. I was an agent for them for three years and by the end I had a turnover of £800,000. Goodness knows what it is now but the board decided they wanted the sector "in-house".'

Women have nothing to prove so far as selling is concerned. There are also hundreds of thousands of women who own or share businesses, but statistics all too clearly demonstrate their failure to make a breakthrough into the boardrooms of blue-chip companies. In May 2003, the Women and Equality Unit noted that only just over one in ten non-executive posts in the FTSE 100 companies and one in forty executive posts were held by women. Even more damning, only one of these companies had a woman CEO. In all, only 7.2% of directorships were held by women and 39 firms had no female directors. From experience, I know that women are far, far more capable of building and running a business than ever these figures suggest. Martha Lane Fox's view is that sexism is at the root of under-representation:

> 'Things like women having babies as the reason is a fiction. If a man values having a woman as part of the top team, it doesn't matter if she is having a baby or not; you promote her and put her there and work around some of her family stuff because the value she has created is so high. Structurally this country is still geared more towards men than women in business, although not in some other ways. Sometimes women don't help themselves. Because of lack of confidence or failure to promote their causes, they do not work their way up as quickly as they ought to if they want the next breakthrough. Even so, if more chief executives believed that it would create more value in the company to have a half-male and half-female team, it would happen.
>
> 'Being a leader in a business is all about selling the vision, the direction, the dream – whatever those may be – to customers and yourself. I can honestly say in myself it is a real belief in what lastminute.com are doing but it is also partly about upbringing. I had very social parents. From a young age I was always encouraged to involve people and talk to people and be someone who is socially adept. I don't know if I am, but that is certainly what I have been trying to achieve. Not that I would ask my father's advice about business – he'd start talking about preparing for my pension.
>
> 'Every day, every single day, I meet sexism. I don't think if you are a man you can understand at all, having someone slightly, consciously or subconsciously, talking to you in a different way because you are female, or thinking that they need to explain something in a slightly different way, or taking a bit longer to think that you might be a credible person, or all of those things every day. I ignore it, try to show what I am as a person and not get too hung up on it. I would rather make that person feel stupid about what they were thinking than pick them up on it.
>
> 'My mother taught me a very good thing: that it was much better to get your enemies to fall in love with you than hate you – you are in a much stronger position. I am sure Brent will tell you there have

been times I have explained that things make me really angry. Often it occurs when I am with Brent and an investor or potential supplier who will ask a question. I'll answer it, or I will ask a question and the guy concerned will answer it, and continue to look at Brent as if he were a ventriloquist. Over the past two years it has improved as my personal credibility has risen. Or maybe it is because our business credibility has improved. I feel in a very lucky position but absolutely you have to work harder as a woman.

'When you think about it, the lack of women in boardrooms is a terrible waste of talent because we are excellent at being task-focused and delivery-focused and we are equally good at moving on to the next thing. It's hard to say what Brent saw in me; at first I suppose he recognized that I was a particular kind of technical visionary. Brent is the webby person – he really loves the technology. I understand it but it is not the technology that turns me on, it is what we can do for customers. It's so hard to say what I have brought to the business, though I guess where I am good is that if he has a thousand ideas, I can pick a hundred and make them happen. Also a lot of what the brand is came from me. In the early days I wrote all the text on the website, I wrote all the weekly e-mails, and the sort of tongue-in-cheek attitude our brand has comes from me. The incredible technical functionality comes from Brent.'

Martha mentioned lack of confidence in many women as a significant cause of their absence from boardrooms. There is another way to attain a place there: found your own company. After TV-AM failed to renew her contract, despite the success of her Roland Rat character, Anne Wood spent eight months of unemployment attending business courses, pre-paring herself for forming a company, a move which, with her record of innovative children's television work, would have been obvious to an outside observer, but it made her nervous. Eventually Channel 4 made up her mind for her. They said they wanted stories around her new character, Pob, to be independently produced and so she was more or less obliged to form a production company to make and sell her pro-grammes. She named it Ragdoll, in honour of Jemima, her daughter's favourite, and began to operate from the family home in Harborne, Birmingham, which was also security on a bank loan. It took courage to do that and Anne, aided only by a part-time secretary, made minimal profits despite the cult success of *Pob*, who first appeared in 1985, and of a variety of other series, such as *Playbox*, *Storytime* and the *Magic Mirror*. Anne, whose father was a road worker, was brought up in a small coalmining village, Tudhoe, near Spennymoor in County Durham. She described the founding of Ragdoll:

> '*I had the commission from Channel 4 and I didn't raise the money; I had to put our house on the market as security to the bank. It meant I couldn't borrow against the business for anything other than the Pob idea as we had no money – we had the family home and two children in further education.*
>
> '*My husband Barry has always been supportive. Had he not been paying the mortgage I could not have taken the risks I took in a free-lance career. We have had very little money all our lives and we were very North-East-ish, old-fashioned, about it – if you didn't have it you didn't spend it. We had a joint bank account because it was the way I could set up this business and he could pursue his career. I had to then teach myself the difference between being employed and being a freelance. You run a business and if something goes wrong you go bankrupt. With the house as security, it had to work.*
>
> '*I had to start buying in facilities but they were very supportive at Hillside where we did the Pob programme but I think if I hadn't had the track record and also done Roland Rat, which was commercially very sound, it might have been very difficult to sell our ideas and to get commissions. To begin with, anyone starting a business is bound to make a lot of mistakes and the first one I made was not to real-ize there was no real money in the business of doing independent programmes. What turned our fortunes was the sudden rise of the video market, which happened around the time I did Rosie and Jim. But I created Rosie and Jim for Central Television, who then sold it as a video, making £1m and I didn't get a penny of it. I learned from that, yes, I learned a lot from that.*'

In another chapter Anne explains why she believes starting a business in her fifties was successful and beneficial. By coincidence, Dawn Airey also worked at Central Television in Birmingham, and competing for the better slots for her company productions in the independent network – an uncivilized version of selling – was a close equivalent to horse trading in a fifteenth-century gipsy camp:

'It was difficult for a time there because I had gone from being a trainee to controlling programme planning. In other words I was head of schedules, responsible for scheduling programmes in the right slot in order to maximize ratings and revenue.

'These were the days when everything was done by committee, and there were five big companies: London Weekend, Thames, Granada, Yorkshire and Central. There was a network budget assigned by the network controllers to those five companies, so these five directors of programmes had their budgets decided and it was up to them to decide between themselves what shows were going to be commissioned. They would then hand over to the schedulers, whose job was to fit programmes into the schedule. The commissioning, though, didn't always meet the needs of the schedule and so the schedulers had to try to sort out the mess.

'Next week there would be a meeting of the network controllers and basically they would finally decide on what was going ahead. We collectively scheduled the network as well as regional slots so we were there to fight for the slots for our company production. Everyone wanted to inherit the audience from Coronation Street and we all plotted to get that. The two most powerful schedulers came from where there was real competition in the market, London Weekend and Thames, so the planner for London Weekend and the planner for Thames were demigods, and you would have to wine and dine them and drink them under the table to try to get what you wanted. It sort of worked as a process, although now it is streamlined.

'The guys in the '80s doing this job were all in their mid-forties, all men, and they had all worked their way up. Suddenly they had to cope with a woman saying: "You should think about this," and "Maybe you should do it like this." I think going down like a cup of *sick was probably a good analogy – they were pretty hostile. It was quite interesting, when they called me a ****. What they didn't know was that I had been to a boys' public school, so I thought: "These are the rules of engagement, I don't necessarily sink to these rules but I know where you are coming from."'*

Not for the first time, quite by accident Dawn was stepping where angels feared to tread, and, as we continue to discover, once one woman has made the initial breakthrough, others follow. While the media may not be open house for women, finding them in high positions is now commonplace. Dame Marjorie believes the same process will occur in business in Britain and I am sure that time will show she is correct. She points to the US as an example and calculates that our country is five or ten years behind. I strongly disagree with her here, however. To begin with, our culture is nothing like as commercially oriented as America's, and neither is there much active encouragement of women who would like to own or run businesses. They are not helped by the habit of many women intellectuals who think of women in business as 'trade', in much the same manner as the landed aristocracy once regarded entrepreneurs. For those of us in executive positions, changing this state of affairs is the biggest selling job of all. Back to Dawn, who was, typically, the trailblazer. Just how frightful this was, she explained:

'I was a scheduler for a number of years and some other women came onto the group as it got larger; in the end there were three. But before that it had been a pretty horrible time, relentless in terms of brutality in being opposed to ideas, and also the language and drinking. I wasn't deterred, I didn't burst into tears all the time or become a shrinking violet; I just made sure I was good at what I did and I kept persisting. I was quite forceful and told them what I thought. A barrage of abuse was hurled across the table but, fine, I won some of the skirmishes. I came through okay but it was quite horrible in some respects.

'Not all people could cope with it, though. I love what I do and I am passionate about what I do, but ultimately it is only work. We are on this earth for a very short time and it is not about how we do,

it is about what we do and how we live our lives. I don't think it's about what you achieve, either – surely it is about being happy and enjoying what we do. Work is not the be-all-and-end-all, so keep things in perspective.

'I would say to a woman breaking into a business that she has to be self-confident, be true to herself and never exchange who she fundamentally is for what she feels she should be or the organiza-tion should be. You can improve yourself through learning, but don't forget who you are and what motivates you. Don't feel that you ever should change that, because the moment you do you will be found out.'

Known as 'Marge-in-Charge', Dame Marjorie is that single woman chief executive in the *Financial Times* Top 100 companies. And in part it is because her company, Pearsons, includes ownership of the *FT* in a group with a £4bn turnover, that she is also consistently nominated as the world's most powerful businesswoman.

Breaking down the old prejudices

She echoed Dawn in her view that business is only a part of life and not all of it. She commented: 'At our newspaper in Georgia we learned about the importance of having great people, creating a good product, treating customers with respect, and all kinds of other lessons that I've found essential along the way. And most of all we learned that failure isn't fatal. I'd have to say that's the greatest lesson I've learned anywhere so far.' An American from Texas, her husband and former lawyer Albert, bought the newspaper, which won the Pulitzer Prize, and then sold it to a group of businessmen. They managed a family of three children as she rose through the Economist group to take over at Pearsons six years ago. In my talk with her she was optimistic that the impact of women in business would grow. She said:

'I think fundamental change after an era of discrimination takes a while. How many black people are running businesses in the developed world? Not more than women. I do believe we're now in a time when there is no longer a pervasive view that a women is not as good in business as a man, and as that prejudice dies more women will float to the top (or struggle to the top, more likely). The business world is now much more results-oriented, and the old boys' network, while it sometimes still gets the benefit of the doubt, can't sustain its members when they don't produce. The person who can produce gets the job.'

There are plenty of women, and men too, who believe, with Martha Lane Fox, that the government ought to offer some positive discrimination in the way of financial incentives to accelerate the process of bringing more women into business. There is no shortage of women who are prepared to be independent. In May 2003, the Women and Equality Unit calculated that women comprised 26% (824,695) of the 3.2 million self-employed in the UK and further research showed that 24% of men were actively engaged in entrepreneurial activity compared with 11% of women. In their Entrepreneurship Monitor study, the Department of Trade and Industry also found that men in the UK are over 200% more likely than women to start a business. This gulf between men and women business owners remains constant whether or not they are involved in bringing up children. Compare these statistics, though, with those from the US, where 87% of their biggest companies have at least one woman director, while in Britain only one in twenty of the FTSE 100 companies include women as main board directors – confirmation, I think, of my reaction to Dame Marjorie's optimism. But I sincerely hope that she is right and I am wrong.

Every respected test of academic ability shows that women are at least the equal of men and, while the genetic make-ups are different and some women are prepared to suspend or even sacrifice a career for motherhood – I have absolutely no criticism of this – the figures above represent a scandalous waste of talent for the improvement of standards at upper levels of management.

It only emphasizes the sentiment first expressed nearly a century ago by Henry Higgins who, in *My Fair Lady*, the musical version of George Bernard Shaw's play *Pygmalion*, sings 'Why can't a woman be more like a man?' It is a prejudice at the heart of the problem that reveals itself in the lack of impact that women are still having at the highest levels. Until we break free from the attitude that a woman must mentally out-muscle the male – the Margaret Thatcher syndrome – the task of achieving equality of opportunity will continue to be a very tough sale indeed.

Key lessons

- *If you want to be an entrepreneur you must be able to sell; whether its selling yourself, your ideas, your products or your dreams!*
- *Convincing the doubters of your faith in your own abilities is a great way to earn yourself respect quickly. Don't be put off by the doubters and the sceptics.*
- *Being a great salesperson is also about spotting new opportunities before anyone else does. You will need to learn to 'smell' a new prospect and back your conviction to the hilt.*
- *By following your instincts and working with conviction and passion, you will undoubtedly do your bit to break down the prejudicial barriers along the way.*

CHAPTER

5

under the (media) spotlight

Dawn Airey and Sly Bailey are high-powered, front-page profile women who have outpaced their contemporaries in the media business. As a former advertising director myself, I know that the barriers to women have largely been removed in newspapers and television, so there is only a slight surprise element in that Dawn is MD of SkyTelevision and Sly is chief executive at the Trinity Mirror group of newspapers, Britain's biggest with the *Mirror* stable among the national red-tops and Trinity with a conglomerate of provincial dailies, evenings and weeklies.

At Sky, Dawn can afford to be expansionary and adventurous, challenging the network stations with all manner of Rupert Murdoch brands in a bid to win 10% of the television audience. Sly has a different agenda altogether. While Trinity Mirror is very profitable, the circulation of the *Mirror* half had been in decline for 20 or 30 years and she was brought in as chief executive on the basis that a lot of people had failed to halt the slide and it was time that a fresh, forensic mind was employed to find solutions.

I find her story enlightening, and the contrast between Dawn's advancement and Sly's will be hugely motivating both to women who went through formal education to degree level and to those who did not. Sly learned from experience alone that by confronting the sternest of challenges there was nothing to fear except judging yourself not to have done the very best you could. She has been described in this way: 'Very ballsy, very hard-headed and tough. She knows her mind and is highly driven and highly ambitious. Those who meet her at first might only see the toughness, but she takes time to take people with her and even those who you think might be alienated by her really rate her and respect her.'

Blazing a trail

She is respected so highly, I believe, because she really cares about the people who work with her, in a way so often alien to men. The way, and speed, with which she has risen should be hugely motivating to young women who start work without an idea of a career path. This is how she began her story:

> *'My father was a financial journalist but that had no influence on my career. I was about three weeks in the sixth form at grammar school when I gave up. I was 16, living in London and I had no idea what I wanted to do. I worked in various jobs in travel and retail and I suppose I was going through an unfulfilled, difficult period during which I sort of instinctively knew I could do something but had no idea what the something could be.*
>
> *'One day I saw an advertisement to sell space in* The Guardian. *It didn't actually say what the job was, just that the successful candidate would be working in a fast-moving environment, things like that. I was 22 and because the job sounded like fun I rang up and I was offered an interview, then two more and I was given the job, although I had no idea about it – clueless about what I was to do when I sat at a desk – but I found myself earning £12,500 a year,*

which also suddenly meant I could think about having a car and buying my own flat as I was living at home until then.

'A vista opened up, not from a career perspective but with lots of other things personally. If someone had come up to me and said one day I would be a manager in this department, I would have been gobsmacked, let alone that I would end up running a newspaper. It was extraordinary that such a thing could happen, but I started there and just found that I could do the job, and really in lots of ways I couldn't believe that I was being paid to sell advertising on the phone. Whatever the bottom rung of the ladder is I was one underneath it! I was selling UK holiday advertising to all those lovely people who ran nice places in the UK, and special interest holidays. I used to love talking to them about their businesses and by doing so I would sell them something, and at first I didn't quite understand the link between the two – i.e., the basis of the seller understanding need and then offering something useful to the buyer.'

Sly admits she was lucky to have found a nurturing environment where there was a strong focus on training and bringing out the best in people. I believe that in a lot of business and commerce there is an enormous hole where proper training ought to be, and any aspiring businesswoman should be aware that her greatest resource is the skill of capable and experienced people. The best of them are only too pleased to be able to explain to recruits how particular jobs should be done. Sly was taught well:

'I learned very early on that the more you put into people to help them achieve, the more you will get back for your business. I never had much time for the managers who sat there and thought: "What are you doing? Get on with it. Do more. Do more." Instead I wondered how I could help someone to reach their goals. My attitude was: "Let's work it out. Let's isolate what the issues are and find out…" Because of this, I instilled into myself a sound formula for getting the best out of people.

'I sold advertising for only six months and I was made a manager in the department. I don't think I was one of the best salespeople

they had ever had, but I enjoyed it. I did it and I was a team player and they saw things in me that I had no idea existed. As visionary managers they were brilliant. I could have gone to lots of other news-papers that wouldn't have set me on the right road. I progressed to being one of the managing team in the advertising department and I was successful and I really enjoyed it, but even then I didn't have any ambition to do anything more than working in a place and a job that I loved.'

Those who understand the intimacy of the newspaper business will not be surprised that a rival was suddenly knocking on her door. Sly was called by *The Independent* about six months after its launch and asked to become classified advertising manager. As everyone close to the industry knew, the *Indie's* editorial style had made a big impact on the broadsheet market, but the business side was short, extremely short, on the adver-tising side. They were frank about it and they thought they knew what needed to be done. There is a point in most careers when a life-changing challenge arrives; when the chance comes for you to make your reputa-tion by creating something out of very little. I had it with Birmingham City. Sly had it with *The Independent*. When it comes, look it in the eye, don't blink, and think positively. Don't fear failure. For her, there could be only one decision:

'Ambition was starting to creep in about then. I thought: "I can make a difference. I know I can do this and it sounds like the next chal-lenge." This was really a big thing for me. I loved the environment at The Guardian, so it wasn't through any sense of dissatisfaction – it was just that the challenge became very compelling. The move was typical of everything that has happened to me since. I have never looked for anything; people have come to me, and the more I have looked at how much there is to do, the greater the attraction, the feeling of "I have to do this."

'So I went to The Independent, *having doubled my salary over-night. It made everything fall into place. I was 25 and I guess my three years' experience there was best summed up by my discovery*

that if everything at The Guardian *worked rather like clockwork,* The Independent *was bandit country, like working at a market stall. In many ways it was like learning how not to do things and finding a way to put things right. The classified department was a horrible mess, like working in a bunker. I would look through the newspaper and, although it was a fight against adversity, in many ways I felt it was a joy to be in the bunker: it was a challenge to generate some money from advertising before the 3.00 p.m. deadline each day when we had to wrap up.*

'I had a team of about 35 people working on six issues in a five-day working week. I used to get in every day and everyone would look at me and ask: "What are we going to do today to make some money?" I'd reply on the lines of: "What we are going to do today is…" and it was literally that: there was no money and we were up against it. Rupert Murdoch was defending The Times *and trying to kill our newspaper's circulation and we were trying to create classified marketplaces out of nothing, with no money to market them so readers did not know they were there.*

'Three years of doing that seriously puts concrete in a woman's backbone and I think if I hadn't gone through that experience I probably wouldn't have been able to go on and do many of the things I did afterwards. You just learn to cope with such adversity. Commercially, from the perspective of your product, you learn how to manage people and how to motivate them, not only that but to do so in a hard environment. We created a team and despite all of the downsides I enjoyed every second. It was a fabulous time.'

Having the appetite for a challenge

Her taste for challenges now well developed, another was to come in 1989 when IPC magazines got in touch with her to see if she was interested in setting up another advertising operation. Many women have a person to whom they can turn when they want advice from someone who is firmly on their side. For Sly, it was her father:

'When the approach came, my initial thought-process went something like: "Who are these people in the sleepy world of magazines and why on earth would I want to go and work for them?" The head-hunter tried to persuade me to attend an interview. I have always talked to my dad about everything I have done, so I went to him and we decided it would be as well to go along just to see what they wanted and what they planned to be doing. There might be something to learn.

'So, reluctantly, along I went, and it was like going back in time to the '70s. The reception area was like a backwards time warp. When you walk into a business, you get the vibes and they tell you a lot about what to expect. I went in and I met the chief executive and within 15 minutes my life depended on working for him. And I went from being less than happy about the job to thinking I would do anything for this guy, and that I wanted to work for him as he was so amazing and so inspirational and so clear-sighted about what he wanted – frank about the business and the kind of person he was looking for.

'He wanted someone who could really make a difference and I just thought I must get this job. I didn't know they had a shortlist of six people and I was number six or that they had seen my CV and their thoughts were that I was a "lightweight" compared with the other people who had CVs as long as their arms. The HR director at the time said he thought I might make a Number 2 "if we need one", but John Mellon and I had struck up a bit of chemistry and so I was invited back for a second interview.

'In between them, I took about 20 of their magazines home each night and I worked up a mini-development plan. By the time I attended the second interview I felt I was running the business already. I was soon to have the chance because I got the job. My colleagues said I was mad because the usual route was magazines to Fleet Street, not the other way round. IPC was small, they added, and I would get buried and no one would hear of me again. That wasn't the problem – the problem was opposition to change and if I had known this at the time I might not have accepted.'

People with ambition are not to be penned in. Once they are in control of their own area, they begin to look elsewhere. A square of a picture may be interesting but in time it is the whole canvas that attracts the attention. So it was with Sly. She describes John Mellon as 'the mentor in her life' and his instant deduction that she should head part of the advertising department had been so astute that five years later, at 31, she was appointed to the board.

'They could see that after five years I needed to play a bigger part in the running of the business and they kept giving me more things. John would call me in now and then and say: "We want you to look at this." I would say: "I don't know anything about it," and he would say: "Exactly. Go away and tell me what you think we should be doing." I kept hoovering up different bits of problems and so he put me on the board. I was in advertising, young and a woman – there was one other on the board – and it sent shockwaves through the organization.

'About halfway through my first board meeting, I became aware of how trivial most of it was, so I asked: "Why can't we talk about circulation, not petrol expenses?" That gives an idea of where the company was. By 1997, I was running most of the advertising within IPC but I wanted more responsibility for the actual magazines. I remember the finance director said to me one day: "Where do you see yourself going?" I said: "Actually, John's job," because I had realized by then I wanted to continue onwards and upwards.

'I had not had a thorough education and I asked if IPC would send me to business school on a very financially oriented course, as I felt some parameters were missing. I went to Kellogg's in Chicago for a month, away from the media business. On the flight over there I was nervous, thinking I was going to be found out. On the course were people from Hyatt hotels, engineering companies, Kodak, all sorts of businesses, and I quickly realized that: "Yes, I am as good as they are; I just reached here by a different path." It taught me things and it was important for my confidence as well.'

Striking out

Sly was becoming restless. She had ideas and ambition, and this included having more responsibility. She could have remained silent about it but that wasn't her way. Rather, she sat down with Mike Matthews, who had taken over from John Mellon, and explained to him that, while it was no manner of a threat, it might be time to part amicably when she found a suitable challenge. He listened, made no comment and then shortly afterwards split the biggest division into two, putting all the women's magazines into one package and the three television listings weeklies into another, which Sly was to run. The three titles – *TV Times, What's on TV* and *TV and Satellite Weekly* – were the biggest profit contributors. Sly said:

> 'It wasn't as though I had suddenly to manage a huge portfolio, but people were asking whether the magazines had a long-term future because of all the listings in newspapers and elsewhere. TV Times' circulation was dropping almost as if the strategy was to drive it downmarket and kill the profit. I had inherited a report that the business was run in a very hierarchical way, but I like flatter structures where I can work more closely with people, so I got there on my first day and no one came to see me. I was sitting in a room all by myself, not surprisingly as only one person reported directly to me. I thought: "I can't run the business like this", so I made some fundamental changes to the structure and had the editors reporting direct to me as a means of getting in there and running the business.
>
> 'It was a great time. We took the business to its highest circulation market share, put TV Times back into growth after three periods of 10% decline. We put into place more rigorous disciplines of work, researched readership and consumers' needs, and began a massive turnaround. People have a great passion for TV and great publishing ideas came out of that.'

Then Christmas was cancelled for several directors in 1997, when over the holiday period they staged a management buyout of IPC in two weeks, after it had been announced the business was for sale. They paid £860m but Sly admits: 'We were still wet behind the ears.' Thus began an extraordinary chapter in which she became boss of the company. It began in a downbeat way.'

Another problem was that Mike Matthews wanted a stand-alone company and when the venture capitalists asked him how we planned to bring this about he didn't really know. He was an implementer not a strategist. The upshot was that we did not do much at all, we were heavily criticized in the press and our share price halved from the issue price. There was a lot of frustration on the board because we were not doing things we wanted to, and Mike was exhausted – he didn't seem able to cope with the agenda.

'Working for venture capitalists is very different from working for a corporation. You have to lock into their methods and aspirations very quickly, then get on with it and deliver. They have different objectives to being part of a corporate body. During this troubled and frustrating period I began to consider leaving the company. Then on a Saturday morning in October 1999, I took a call at home from David Arculus. I knew something was going on as he had tried to contact me on a Friday night and it was unusual for board members to have a direct relationship with the chairman as he did everything through Mike.

'He said he had two important things to say to me: number one, that Mike Matthews was stepping down as chief executive and number two, that he and Simbon would like me to run the company. I was absolutely stunned. He asked whether I could talk about it at the time and I said that I was about to go to the hairdresser's. Then he suggested we talked that evening but I said I couldn't as I was going to a pop concert. He must have thought it was bizarre that he was offering this big job and I wasn't able to talk about it, but I needed time to reflect and talk to my husband, Peter.

'His view was that I had to do it or leave the company. He said: "You can run that company. You have been frustrated over the last few years and have spoken to me every night for the last two years about what is not being done. You know what you want to do and you have to take the job or leave. You can't just stay there or you

will be a total pain in the backside to someone else." So it was a complete, life-changing conversation for me.

'Next day I talked to David, who hadn't had a particularly good relationship with Mike. I told him I was only going to take the job if he and I worked out the rules of engagement. The company was not well placed, we had a lot to achieve and then we had to have an exit for the business, either by flotation or a sale. It was non-negotiable. It was either that or breaking up, which was an alternative but not the preferred one. I said I knew it was going to be tough and we had to have rules of engagement so that if the wheels fell off we could put them back on again.'

In the hot seat

That afternoon the pair of them met for three hours at the Hilton, Stansted airport, to go into the detail. They set a strategy, discussed their relationship and what Simbon expected, even the PR. Sly took over the business in December 1999 and the move generated extraordinary interest, not just in a 37-year-old woman running a media company, but also because she had been involved in the biggest management buyout in UK history.

'I was inundated with calls for interviews and profiles and that sort of thing. I had the whole works. Sly, her fridge, wardrobe, husband and cats was what they wanted! They wanted to concentrate on me being on the younger side, blonde and so forth, whereas it was really about business and focusing on that. In the end we did some business profiles because I wanted to demonstrate with results rather than plans.'

It was the height of the dot.com boom, when many analysts were forecasting that magazines were dying and screen-based reading would take over. Her strategy was to focus the company on five core markets, so they laid out a very clear growth plan and started to deliver it. Profits were up by 22% in the first year, an indication she was going in the right direction, and early in 2001 there were conversations with AOL Time Warner about the sale of the business. She had seen this as the way ahead for IPC, although it was bound to mean that she would lose operational control of the company, a position she had enjoyed. The talks continued for months, first of all in great secrecy, before the final exchange of contracts in June. The price was £1.15bn, and she found herself working for corporate America, and of this experience she said:

> 'I flew to New York every month but I wasn't running the company any longer. I understood why from their point of view, but I didn't want to go to New York and climb the AOL Time Warner ladder. I don't have a portable family anyway. Once you get used to running a stand-alone company, it is hard to do something else. Corporate America works through lots of meetings with lots of people and lots of referrals to other people and I don't respond best in that kind of environment.
>
> 'Over the first year we worked very hard integrating the business and at about the time when no one could accuse me to doing a cut-and-run, I had an approach from Trinity Mirror. I was sent a profile of the company, and once again the more I looked at it, the more I thought: "I have got to do this." Although I didn't fully understand the brand, I knew enough about the company overall to know what needed to be done. You either get that or you don't, frankly. I knew that people would say it was the biggest challenge in media, and that is exactly what attracted me.

Onwards and upwards

> 'I met Sir Victor Blank, the chairman, and within three minutes I felt, as I had with David Arculus, that we would have a relationship based on good chemistry between us. I went to the final interview panel with a very clear document in terms of what I believed needed to be done with the business and my guarantees as to how I would tackle it. If they didn't want that, then they had better pick someone else. That night they rang me and said: "You have the job."

'I was euphoric. Twenty years at Harvard Business School could not teach you what going through a management buyout does and I just felt that I was ready to run a plc. It was the logical step – to manage a great media company – although it certainly had, and still has, issues. It has been all I wanted it to be and we are starting to make progress. My wish is to lead and manage, but it is the team who make things happen and we now have the right people.

'As for my time at IPC, it is almost like I have put it away in a lovely box and tidied up. It has wonderful memories but someone asked the other day if I missed IPC, and it is strange but I don't even think about it.'

Dawn Airey is the product of a boys' school that was kind enough to allow girls in, no doubt as much for the chance to ensure profitability by doubling potential intake as for any notion of equality. But who knows? Unlike Sly, Dawn went to university: Cambridge. She is one of three children and had a mildly unconventional but happy upbringing, highly structured with every evening filled with sport, drama, or some form of class. She, too, fell into a career after a few years of fending off responsibility to anything but her youthfulness. She has the same kind of driven personality and dynamism as Sly and she still prefers co-operation to confrontation. She said:

'I did geography at Cambridge because I enjoyed the subject, but before going there I travelled the world on and off for two years. It was the late '70s, and the vogue then was to go to Israel and work in a kibbutz, so that's what I did. Then I went to Egypt and pottered around the Middle East having an absolute ball. I decided I loved it so much I wanted to continue travelling, but I didn't have the money. My father would not send me a cheque, so I returned to the UK and worked at a NatWest Bank in Plymouth during the day, a pub in the evening and a vet's at the weekend so that I could quickly amass as much money as possible.

'After three months I continued travelling for nine months and then went to Cambridge. Geography wasn't hugely demanding so I had plenty of time to do other things I enjoy, including playing tennis, *running the university rag, sitting on the students' advisory council for the Cambridge Union and on my common room council, and lots of other stuff. I see it now as a big rehabilitation from my trauma of school. It was a lovely course with lovely people at a lovely college, and all along I knew I wanted to go into TV or newspapers.'*

Being turned down by the BBC for its general trainee course upset Dawn but she was soon writing to all the commercial stations. The single reply she received was from Central Television in Birmingham. They asked her to attend an interview and it was there that she was soon to find a mentor in Andy Allen, the director of programmes, who, although she was not to know it for eight years, had been instrumental in offering her a traineeship.

'I had gone through the interview procedure and right at the end of it I had to meet the board, including Bob Phillips, the chief executive. They asked lots of questions about what I watched and, because I had done my homework, I knew that at the time the headquarters in Broad Street, Birmingham, was a real powerhouse, producing stuff like Boon, Crossroads, *and* Spitting Image. *I was a bit, I won't say saucy, but I was, well, I like to engage in conversation and maybe I pushed the boundaries a little bit, but it was fun and I had them laughing.*

Dare to be different

'I took a phone call next day saying I had the job, but first they wanted to send me to a psychologist. I put the phone down and I thought: "Shit, I wonder if it is about me." I phoned them back and asked whether everyone was subject to this psychologist visit. The reply was: "Yes, all four of you are going down." I thought: "Four? There are only three positions." So obviously one of us was going to be knocked out.

'I spent a day with this psychologist in Bristol and I never knew what he had to say about me. There were a lot of obvious questions

like: "What is your relationship like with your father?" I thought it was a stupid bloody question. I treated it with the contempt it deserved and thought nothing more of it. I started at Central in the January and it was only at my leaving do eight-and-a-half years later that the wonderful Andy said: "You don't know this, but what we are going to do is read what that psychologist had to say about you eight years ago." It said in summary: "Dawn Airey is the highest risk candidate. She will either be a fantastic success or she will alienate everybody. We cannot predict, and you have to make the decision." So Andy said: "We made the decision to employ you because you made us laugh."

'*So there you are. Andy was brilliant. I joined Central as a trainee.*'

It was true she was being trained but was not sure for what. As in Sly's case, Dawn embarked on the journey without a clue as to her destination. But quality shines through, especially if it comes with dynamism and a positive attitude. Her creed as expressed below could stand for that of hundreds of high-flying women.

'*I have never been a careerist; I do what I enjoy and I think if you do that and you are bright and you work that bit harder than anyone else, you are going to get on. And it is funny I should keep going back to Andy, because in many ways he was my mentor. He told me: "The difference between you and other people is that other people bail out, you just roll up your sleeves and keep going. You just get it done." I think that probably comes from my dad, who would say to me that if I was going to do it with all odds stacked against me, and if that comes easy, then great. He has been a guiding light throughout my career.*

'*I like to think I am nice to work for. What I expect from a boss is someone who can give you leadership and vision and add to what you do sometimes, but also be very supportive. That is how I am to those people around me. You should treat people with respect and give them latitude; treat them as intelligent human beings, while being aware that intelligent human beings make mistakes. When you understand why the mistake happened you should be supportive and understanding. Ultimately, it is not the end of the world. I have always employed good people around me – always – and in fact people I have employed in individual areas are better than I have ever been. If you employ people who want your job and are brilliant at what they do, you are only going to benefit from it. I never, ever feel undermined by having brilliant people around me after my job. That is exactly what I want – I go searching them out.'*

Inner belief

As Dawn added, this attitude amounts to an expression of self-confidence. Without inner belief, no one can be a good leader. Women are prone to having their confidence undermined and I would love to believe that this book helps some of them discover within themselves the resilience to go and do what they believe they are good at. Leadership is not defined by loudness and brashness – often the very opposite: it is that quiet certainty that, through good times and bad times, you will come through with your knowledge increased and, as Sly put it, with concrete in your backbone. Dawn is also self-aware:

'I know what my failings are. I know how I can be wound up and I know how one's temperament can affect people around you. I am not an early bird; I hate getting up early. Anything before 8.30 and I am barely civil, but I work late and at weekends too. These are long hours but most people at this level do them – it goes with the territory. You don't get paid decent money for sitting on your backside all day – and that is fine!

'If you are in a leadership position and have had a terrible day for whatever reason, you shouldn't go out and make everybody aware

of it. That's not to say that you are a cipher: you must always be true to who you are and you can't pretend to be something that you are not, as you'll be caught out. I am very happy to take risks. I don't for one minute think I have all the answers and I am not afraid of making decisions. Why am I successful? It is probably that I make more decisions and I get more things right than I get wrong. Just give me the stuff, I'll make decisions all day every day if you want me to; I am certainly not afraid of making decisions. I am quick and speedy at doing what I do, but I am not interested in doing production work myself any more – I am more interested in facilitating and finding where we need to go.'

Now, from her very senior position, she goes out of her way to spot talent, another sign of great maturity in a business leader and, the higher an executive rises, the more important it becomes to prepare a legacy for the company. These might be in sound business structures, in the best buildings and equipment, or in staff and shareholder satisfaction but, ultimately, there is no legacy to rival that of outstanding people at every level. Dawn added:

'I have always been very fortunate in the people I have chosen, and I can think of only two I have been unable to recruit when I wanted to. Both times it was because they were so new into the job they were doing that they did not feel that they could leave. I can pretty much employ anyone I want, which is a nice position. I have got a good crop of brains around me.

'As for my career, it has been quite linear, but if you enjoy what you do and do it well somebody will come along and offer you something irresistible, and if it is irresistible you can't resist it. If it is resistible, continue doing what you are doing, which is certainly what has happened to me and to quite a few of my colleagues. You are happy doing what you are doing and somebody comes along and says: "Do you fancy doing this?" Well, I always like learning and I don't mind going out of my comfort zone to learn something. Sky is the biggest stretch in my professional career I have ever had. I have

been here only a few months and I am getting jobs done, under-standing the organization structure, getting to know people.'

People reach the top, and stay there, by going the distance, by making and taking tough decisions. Sly and Dawn are proving that women have all that it takes to conquer mountains and to inspire other women to follow them on the climb.

Key lessons

- *Even without formal training or a business education, you can learn an awful lot from rolling up your sleeves and actually getting on with it, and by listening to the best ideas of the people around you.*
- *When a great opportunity looks you in the eye, don't look away, but grab the chance while it's still there.*
- *If you suddenly find yourself thrust into the hot seat, be wary not to forget and trust the instincts that got you there in the first place.*
- *Dare to be different. It may just be what makes you stand out from the crowd.*
- *If you continually challenge yourself, and relish what you do, you will find that other new and exciting opportunities will come your way.*

6

winning against the odds

Anne Wood's story must be one of the most inspirational in this book. Not because she overcame insuperable odds to succeed, although they were high enough; not because she battled her way to fame from unpromising beginnings, although she did that too; but because she made the best of disillusioning circumstances and built a famous production company employing dozens of talented people for the good of millions of children across the world. Some record from a woman who was close to her 50th birthday when she founded her company, Ragdoll.

Anne is in the second half of her sixties now but the passion to create remains and the business brain, about which she is modest at times to the point of denial, has been honed to sharpness by a succession of what she calls mistakes, but which were actually the result of a lack of awareness of the opportunities for a woman of her exceptional talents. The first of these was the loss of as much as £1m in revenue because of an unpredicted, and possibly unpredictable, spread of the video market at the turn of the 1990s. She proved then that she could fight back, that she could be tough and resilient and not surrender to her fate.

Some businessmen would say that what separates the men from the girls is the ability to take it on the chin and come back. It sounds like a vast generalization to me, but successful women are marked above all else by determination, and it takes a great deal of determination, even a degree of obstinacy, to push on regardless of the blows that can come raining in.

Determination is Anne's middle name. Her story underlines the fact that before success you will meet temporary defeat or even total failure. The easiest thing to do is quit and that's what the majority do. But Anne picked herself up, brushed herself off and got back to work – through sheer determination to overcome set backs, problems and failures.

Showing what you are made of

With Anne, this was true from the beginning because with her background, as she says, she was either going to become a nurse or a teacher. She chose teaching because she loved books and children, and eventually combined the two, first to create imaginary characters to whom children could relate and then, as a reluctant entrepreneur, to turn them into a worldwide phenomenon. *The Teletubbies*, designed for the under-twos – a market that previously existed only for clothing, toys and food – has been translated into 44 languages and watched in 113 countries, and Tinky Winky, Dipsy, Laa-Laa and Po are her superstars.

She had an independent streak from the beginning. Brought up in a colliery town near Spennymoor, County Durham, she was the only surviving child, her mother having lost three boys. Her father was a road worker and Methodist lay preacher and the family fell precisely into the 'respectable working class' bracket. From grammar school she went to a teaching college in Bingley, a suburb of Bradford in Yorkshire, but not to university because, she says: 'I felt my parents couldn't afford it and, from this great distance, if I am honest, because I felt socially inferior.' Anne added:

'For girls from the North East, the home of Andy Capp, the expectations were not there and the greatest crime of all, one that I think

infects women in many places even today, is the lack of expecta-
tion, the lack of feeling and opportunity. Nobody at school actually
pushed me. I was driven by my interest in children. In her later years,
my mother used to say to my father: "Where does she get it from?"
and he used to reply: "It is books, woman, books." They tried to
figure it out because I was a bit of a cuckoo in the nest. Of course, if
you didn't go to university and you were bright, you either became
a teacher or a nurse. The obvious thing for me was to be a teacher
because I read anything I could get my hands on – magazines, pic-
ture postcards, nothing deliberately educational really. I could never
get enough books to read, and I suppose you are always working for
the child you were.'

One of the great skills of business is to spot a market. As a teacher of
English at a secondary modern school, to which children who failed the
11-plus were sent, Anne was bothered early on that children could read
but had no popular paperbacks to turn to. Then, with the development
of printing technology in the '50s, it became possible to publish glossy
picture books and mass-produce inexpensive paperbacks. She recognized the opportunity and became one of the first editors at Scholastic,
who sold children's paperbacks in schools. This sales strategy was not
looked upon with favour by a lot of teachers, who accused the company
of being 'nasty commercial'. Anne said: 'You sell a Teletubby doll and
you are a "nasty commercial", whereas the reality of children's lives is
that they are living in a commercial world.'

This is, I think, a revealing comment because in the business climate I
would like to help bring about – one in which women from any environment and upbringing would not instinctively disqualify themselves or
be disqualified – she might have become a children's publisher herself,
because she understood that culture and commerce are perfectly com-
patible. No matter, she soon left her job to start her family and, inevitably
at the time, gained an introduction to television through *Bill & Ben* and
Watch With Mother. She did not know it then – indeed, she admits that
she would have laughed at anyone suggesting television or publishing

was to be her future – but by such stealthy methods building blocks are put into place.

Anne slipped into television by a side-door. When she left teaching – in between looking after her children, washing, ironing and doing the housework – she remained an editor, then began conceiving ideas for authors and what she calls 'writing about children's stories in the educational press', which, I suspect, means she was a critic. She recalls:

'This work coincided with the early days of Jackanory and the first programmes reviewing children's books. From being a consultant editor, I began to publish my own work as a journalist and then formed an association of parents who wanted to know more about children's books, called Books for Your Children, and this led to a national organization of parents. I continued along this path until 1976, when I was asked to become a consultant at Tyne Tees television, which developed into a production job because they didn't know how to use consultants up there.

'So suddenly I was lumbered with producing a programme and it was panic stations. Television people held the rather patrician view that a child would just sit and watch a programme with mother: that was until TV-AM came along and I was head of children's programmes there. My philosophy is that you can understand the character you create if you know what you want to see at the end. I always have had a very clear idea of why kids like a character and what it is they like.

'I am also fascinated by what is the difference between a childhood perception and an adult perception, and how the two come together. And how does one affect the other and how does the culture of children arrive? It arrives from the interaction between the conception of the world and the adult world they find themselves in. So they observe the contemporary and they take it back into their own culture and transform it. Today, with rapid, computerized images, things are changing at a breakneck speed. From Tyne Tees I went to Yorkshire Television to do The Book Tower and that won all kinds of awards. Adapting all those books and doing Ragdolly

Anna, I had learned my trade. I brought pre-school to the top of the agenda and if there is one thing I am proud of it is that I focused the importance of television on early learning.'

It was at TV-AM that Anne introduced the world to Roland Rat, originally as a mickey-take of people who took themselves and children's programmes very seriously. She says:

'I just thought it would be funny to have a rat in children's TV. I think it touched a nerve because when this rat came up and said: "Good morning, children," it was so funny, people wanted to smile. I think I have always been a bit naughty. Then Greg Dyke took over and although he wanted to change a lot of things he decided to keep Roland and, in fact, we put the rat on the road in a pink Austin A40, travelling to different locations. We also started a Sunday morning programme called Rub-a-Dub-Tub, which was so popular with kids their parents called it their "nookie hour".

'When Greg Dyke left, he was replaced by an Australian, Bruce Gyngell, who has since died. His brief was to maintain the high ratings but increase profits by cost-cutting, and I was one of the victims. He replaced my productions with imported cartoons linked live in the studio. It was unlucky for me because, where other people who had been true to the station were on high contracts and left with loads of money, I who had done more than most to keep it going was just left to depart. Then I found that although I had been highly successful no one wanted to employ me. I learned one or two things, though. I thought right then that if I had to start a company I would remember that if I had money for every Roland Rat balloon and doll that had been sold I wouldn't be starting out with nothing, so I did keep the character rights from the beginning.'

So she was out on her own, nearly 50, with only her book work, her experience of running departments and her husband's income to back the initiative she had been forced to take when the recently born television company, Channel 4, told her they would only commission her new idea direct from her. The concept was *Pob's Programme* and so, in 1984, she put forward her home as security and formed Ragdoll Productions (UK) Limited, working from that same home. Of this fraught time, she says:

> '*I am the most reluctant to talk about money. I get embarrassed when I am put on the spot about it. Anyway, I had the commission but I couldn't raise the money. I had to put our house on the market, our family home, which meant that I couldn't borrow against the business for anything other than that idea as we had no money – we just had the family home and two children in further education. My husband, who was a buyer for ITV, has always been supportive. Had he not been paying the mortgage, I don't know what we would have done.*
>
> '*Being out of work for 18 months was a terrible experience. I tried very hard not to form this company, partly because I had been running a magazine on children's books for a long time and I didn't want to finish doing that, and partly because I knew how difficult it would be to produce programmes and do the business side of things. There were many factors involved and I spent the first year really trying to discover how to sell. The thing is that, as a freelance, if you lose your job as an independent producer you go bankrupt. In the end I just had to do it. I went on a business course and I learned enough to understand things like business plans. I had already picked up SWOT analysis but there were subjects like cashflow cascade that are useful to know about without actually using them day-to-day. I know I made a lot of mistakes, and in the case of Rosie and Jim I wasn't careful enough.*'

For Anne, the missed opportunity of making about £1m on *Rosie and Jim* was a business watershed. From then on, her love for her work and for what it brought to young children was never again going to blind her to the realities or to the fact that, when it comes to making money, no paragraph of small print should be unread. And, yes, she also discovered that sentiment and business do not mix.

Pob was followed by a succession of well-loved programmes for various network companies before, in 1990, *Rosie and Jim*, two ragdolls who live a secret life on a canal boat, found another home in Central Television. Shot on location, the first series of 25 programmes went well over budget and Ragdoll was in crisis, until Central ordered another 25. It is difficult to make ratings for children's programmes because under-fours aren't counted. Nevertheless, Central must have known how popular the *Rosie and Jim* programmes were because video sales boomed to more than a million. Anne still bridles at Central's refusal to divide the profits 50/50:

> 'They would not compensate me and they wanted a second series of the programme, so I said: "Fine. Let us out the overspend on series one into the budget of series two so that I don't lose money," but they wouldn't. Not only that, they took away my production fee, which in those days we used to get to offset against the production cost. That was when the iron entered my soul and I thought: "I will never let anyone ever do this to me again." So then I sat down and took a hard look at everything and I made certain that I never got myself into that situation again.'

Ragdoll had moved from the Wood house in Birmingham, first to Henley-in-Arden and then to Stratford-upon-Avon, where Anne was to set up a shop on the strength of her *Rosie and Jim* profits, and often used the bathroom as an outside filming location. The shop continues to sell her little heroes and heroines in massive quantities – she gave the *Rosie and Jim* doll franchise to Oxfam – while headquarters are now on a lot in a trading estate on the fringe of the town.

From her beginnings, with only a part-time secretary, Anne had appointed some brilliant young talent but, while producing a number of hallmark shows such as *Playbox*, *Storytime* and *The Magic Mirror*, the company never did much more than break even until the video market expanded. When it became an international success, Anne was ready, because, as she said almost plaintively: 'The thing is, I have become this person who knows a bit through experience but I didn't set out to do it.'

Tina Blake, who did some freelance work for Anne, was full of admiration for the way she included everyone in her projects, and she picked up a tip or two about how to bargain. Anne tried a *quid pro quo* on a freebie video in exchange for the high profile Tina would get on *Rosie and Jim*. Of the dealings, Anne says:

> *'She got her high profile, but what I really wanted to do was involve other people and there's nothing I wouldn't do to bring that off. I am passionate about elevating the standards of material for children. Whether you are talking about a businessman or a diva or whatever, you must have a passion for what you do. In my experience, I haven't found anyone who is truly successful at what they do who doesn't love what they do.'*

Further evidence of Anne's financial acuity came in 1990 with her deal to produce *Brum* for the BBC. It is the story of a little car who has exciting adventures in Birmingham, still probably the car capital of England. The persuasive Anne talked the City Council into giving the series its financial support and it has certainly been repaid many times in publicity terms, although the first two sets of 26 programmes in all, narrated by Toyah Willcox, was not a big profit-maker. However, a technologically advanced second series, with Brum as much more of a zany superhero, has sold to 41 countries, including, crucially, the US, where Ragdoll's company visibility through *The Teletubbies* had opened doors. Indeed, the endearing *Brum* is set to become second only to *The Teletubbies* as a Ragdoll earner.

Pushing the boundaries

Thus I have encapsulated a decade of hard work and sparkling imagination into a few sentences. Anne's next contribution shows just how many vital decisions have to be made in this competitive industry. When the BBC asked 12 companies to tender for a daily pre-school series, she had strong doubts about whether Ragdoll had the production resources for such a massive commission, even though the brilliant *Tots TV* for Central had twice been voted Young Children's Programme of the Year, was being shown in 50 countries and had made the company's US break-through on the Public Services Broadcasting Channel. It is history now that Ragdoll won the commission only an hour before Anne took off for the US to try to sell it there. Did this woman ever stop!

> *'The BBC were interested because they had watched how successful* Rosie and Jim *and* Tots TV *were, but they wouldn't just commission us – they put us on a limited tender list. To go every day on BBC was a massive decision and I was really in two minds. Was I tough enough?'*

Anne had become aware through years of cold-calling in the US that often it wasn't what you were but who you knew. Her annual visits to television headquarters in New York and Washington had caused no response, so she attacked the problem from another direction, and in a way that was relatively inexpensive. Her idea was to organize a programme exchange and so at the 1992 MIPCOM TV market Ragdoll invited a number of international producers to take part in an exchange of five-minute, non-dialogue films featuring a young child in a home environment. In the years since, the company has co-ordinated dozens of films from 27 countries. Even more satisfying was the success in America. She says:

> *'The only way we would survive was by having an international profile and a brand identity, because you weren't seen as having made the programmes.* Tots TV *went out on Central Television but although we made it completely by ourselves we were in danger of being invisible behind the station name, as independent producers have a tendency to be. I did two things, I opened a Ragdoll shop, which at first was known locally as the* Rosie and Jim *shop, and I focused on selling internationally. This is much more difficult than it seems and I shall always be indebted to old Breskie at PBS for help-ing us so much.*

'But, before that, I remember asking the international sales person at Central why they hadn't sold abroad, and I had the response: "Your tapes have got more coffee stains on them from being left in more people's offices than any I know." And I said: "Fine. So you have no objection if I take them away from you?" and I started to go to the US myself and I never left the tapes unless I felt someone was going to look at them, although you never quite knew whether they would. I could only afford to go once a year, so I used to try different air routes to Washington and New York. I took Tots TV to Breskie and finally the sale was made. The hardest thing had been going there year after year and being disappointed. I knew the programmes were very good but we just couldn't sell them over there.'

It was making the most of this wonderful opportunity that made the company what it is today. Control of the characters it created had always been Ragdoll's policy even from the days of *Pob* (a lesson learned from Roland Rat), but by 1995 it was clear that to survive Ragdoll needed more financial control as well as creative control and if this meant taking more financial risk as well as creative risk, that was the path that had to be followed. Fortunately, by now the bank had agreed to accept the company's back catalogue as security, rather than the family home, so if the programme failed, all the company faced was insolvency, which was bad enough but not as bad as Anne being homeless.

Holding on to your beliefs

Anne's fortitude and tenacious hold on her beliefs are unusual and the inspiration for this chapter. Others are driven by a perception of justice in fighting powerful forces, as well as having an eye for business. Jacqueline Gold provides a couple of examples of her battles with prejudice, not to mention bureaucracy. The sex industry is unlikely to elicit much sympathy from officialdom in any country, let alone Ireland, where she fought the government when she was refused the right to open an Ann Summers store in Dublin. This is how she told the story:

'I had enormous trouble with the Dublin corporation and so I invited them to send someone over to talk to us. Two men came, one of them was cosmopolitan and flexible and the other seemed all right and talked but never looked at me. He had an acute case of tunnel vision. I asked him if his mind was already made up and he admitted with a blatant "Yes" that it was. There comes a point where negotiation doesn't work and it wasn't going to here because I began to think that his whole objective was to get me to back off. He was most intimidating, not quite with threats, but his attitude. He told me people in Ireland just did not want our kind of business, hinting that even the IRA wouldn't like it. That was really underhand and I have to admit made me very determined indeed. I hate being bullied.

'So we went ahead and opened the store and on the first day we had 10,000 people through the door. That night I went on a big show in Ireland, Friday Night Live, where the audience are closely involved. The chap who had tried to intimidate me was on the right. It was amazing to see the audience turn in our favour but even so we were issued with a writ to close us down. We saw it through to the bitter end and we won in court. I even met the Taoiseach Bertie Aherne when he visited the store. I am not the sort of person to get emotional, to pursue justice for the sake of it, but I believe we were right.'

So Ann Summers was playing a part in the emancipation of women in Ireland! More seriously, kicking Jacqueline around is not to be recommended. The British government tried it too, and finished similarly with a bloody nose. Ann Summers were barred from advertising jobs in Job Centre Plus because the nature of their business did not meet with official approval. Again, necessity and the principle of justice met for her, with the need to free restrictions from her business. As the company spent £250,000 a year on recruitment advertising and was still not reaching some potential employees, she began lobbying the Department of Work and Pensions, which would not relent. So she went to law and in the High Court won a notable victory. 'A fantastic victory for Ann Summers and common sense,' said Jacqueline.

Ricky Rudell won compensation from a company who decided to replace her from within their organization. She led the growth of a company from luxury markets to prominence on the high streets and its treatment of her initially left her isolated and jobless at the age of 50. However, Ricky belongs to the high-octane band of women for whom a quiet life is not even an option. She looked around, tried an idea for developing websites, which she dropped, and was then attracted by the spiralling growth of sandwich businesses, particularly in big provincial cities. Her idea was not only to supply passing or regular trade but also to sell high-quality food by systematically calling on every office, business and factory within a two-mile radius. The daily corporate and board-room trade, she deduced, had barely been touched. Between concep-tion and inception are many pitfalls. However, she managed to find the finance and set about the task. The speed of her success is a tribute to sound planning, experience and hard work. She says:

'I did not want to set up a business for someone to take away, so I designed and helped to create websites but soon realized that it wasn't a business for today but perhaps for ten years down the line. I met a young man who was an area manager for a sandwich company. He wanted to start a business but hadn't the money so, because I had always fancied going into fast food, we agreed to set up the Sandwich Club, for which he would do the day-to-day man-agement and I would open up the corporate side.

'I checked a number of operations and soon realized that even those that were not very well run were producing a profit, making me believe that anyone with a business brain could make a major impact. I took the best from the others and tried to do it better, going for high quality, ultra-cleanliness and very, very short queues because people with a brief lunch period want to be in and out. I don't believe in cutting corners and so the balance between cost and quality is a fine one.

'We began at our first shop in Five Ways, Birmingham, by taking £200 a day and after 18 months it was sometimes up to £2000 a day. The corporate side, which accounts for one-third to a half over-all, is very involved. I bought a map, pinned it on the wall, marked

every single company within two miles, and I suppose initially I sold to 75. We delivered buffet lunches for meetings – the boozy lunch seems to be dying off – and sandwiches for office staff, but although we ask for 24 hours' notice, it's often 9.00 a.m. the same day that orders are phoned in. That makes it difficult and sometimes we have to work feverishly, but that's part of the fun – we never know what is going to happen the next day. The other day, a firm phoned in for 100 bacon and 100 sausage sandwiches and I was appalled when they were told they were too late.

'Friends think I'm crazy because sometimes I'm at work at 5.00 a.m., but I don't mind that – the buzz is starting from nothing and building. I know I am tough with suppliers, making sure we get best prices, but you have to remember we are competing with multiples. I am always looking for better bread at a cheaper price but I won't buy anything that I think is below the top standard. My nature is to see a goal and go for it, but I don't believe I am ruthless – I couldn't tread on anyone or use them. I've met some of those ruthless big-company women and I don't much like them.'

Moving mountains

So what makes a middle-aged business-starter such as Anne or Ricky tick? Maybe they are rare exceptions, but I don't think they should be. If someone smart were to take all the bright, energetic, independent and confident 50-year-olds and give them £10,000 each to run efficient, money-making operations, they would move mountains – and not only of sandwiches. Ricky admits she doesn't like women's clubs or sport very much and would rather create. Here she is again:

'The buzz is to build it from nothing. In my fifties, I'm having a great time, unlike many women, who, having seen their kids leave home, seem almost to lose their reason for existence, becoming depressed and losing self-esteem. Inner confidence is very important. If you have it, you feel you can do almost anything you wish. I believe I

have a good business brain and I know from my early selling days, when I worked for a cigarette-lighter firm, that large companies aren't that efficient.

'I have always wanted to prove something for myself, perhaps because I have always been independent and had my own money. That's probably why I think taking money at the till is the best feeling there is. Most companies take three years to make a profit but we made £27,000 in the first year and will own everything within a few months. The plan now is to set up one big base with small feeder shops nearby. I'm also looking at franchising out my ideas. I wish I had gone into all this 20 years ago because I'm sure I would be a multi-millionaire by now.'

I think she still can be.

Key lessons

- *Difficult beginnings are no reason for not being successful. You will need to learn to take the rough with the smooth.*
- *Don't let your emotions cloud your judgement, and learn from your mistakes.*
- *Persevere even in the tough times if you believe that the only stumbling block is that you need to convince people how good your ideas are.*
- *Always stick to your principles. You will win more friends than enemies if you do.*

the tricks of the trade

When businesswomen sit around a table and are frank with each other about the type of character required to move from self-employment to running a firm of even one or two people, certain topics inevitably arise. Many of these will be financial but, because such important subjects as banks and business plans hardly differ for men and women, only in the final chapter of this book do I attempt to offer even the briefest advice.

There are many ways to run an office, firm or factory. The old mill-owner type – 'Thar shall be doin' it this way and no other' – is now, praise be, practically defunct, although some businesses still have those tendencies. Freewheeling can work in offices where people are creative and/or self-driven by virtue of the jobs they are doing. There are many instances of the chaos to be seen on television's *The Office*, but largely it is better to avoid the embarrassments that occur when a manager wants to be one of the boys.

I prefer a relaxed atmosphere in which people understand exactly what they are supposed to be doing. I am not strong on skirts and suits and ties as a type of 'office uniform' and when I put casual dress forward as a possibility I was surprised by the number of pleas I received from staff who wanted at least a degree of clothing regulation. I would have been perfectly happy for people to work in jeans and sweatshirt if their work was purely internal but the staff voted for uniforms – and, as a way of unifying people and underlining the pride in working at our football club, I cannot fault it.

My staff are first-class, loyal and discreet, and I am delighted to have an open-door policy for my own office. We have meetings every week to review progress and to set new targets. I encourage people to come up with ideas and solutions, but not to moan. If you cannot change something, change your attitude to it. If there are legitimate concerns, that's fine. Whingers and moaners are not welcome because it's a waste of time and energy. We all know that the only reason we are there is to make the company better, and when we cease to do that we cease to contribute.

There are few things more satisfying about being the boss than bringing the best out of people, of challenging them to go beyond it and watching them succeed, often to their own amazement but not mine. I observe staff carefully, looking for those who want to be stretched and handing them tasks that are outside their usual areas. I entirely agree with the sentiment that if you want a job done quickly, ask someone who is busy. Its equivalent for a successful businesswoman is that she will be regularly asked to sit on this board or that commission or panel until, frankly, it becomes too much. The point, though, is that stretching a person is the way of discovering potential for promotion.

There isn't a woman in this book who, as a young and ambitious starter, knowingly turned down a work challenge. I can vouch for that. Eventually, in the maturing process, she will learn to take on the challenges that are important to her and the company, but will never have as much excitement as when she did the impossible all by herself. She will make mistakes and overcome pitfalls and never stop trying to do better. She shouldn't worry, because we have all been there. However, it is possible I can be of some help and so from my personal observations and the experience of others, I offer you some words of advice.

Self-confidence: why faith in yourself will pay off all the time

Nothing is more corrosive to a businesswoman, or anyone else for that matter, than a lack of self-confidence. It is the worm in many a budding career, and without self-confidence you are lost. However, that isn't to say it cannot be recovered – it can.

There are many other ways in which a women's confidence can be undermined, often by the attitude of others. Dawn Airey describes some meetings when she was a programme scheduler with Central Television as 'brutally male' in the bullying, swearing and drinking. Maybe they were designed to humiliate her and maybe not, but she had the perfect antidote: she ignored them.

I realize it's not always easy to do that, but it is definitely the best policy. Martha Lane Fox admits that she boiled inwardly at being bypassed during meetings but used her anger productively by showing how successful she could be. Jacqueline Gold admits to feeling intimidated when she was in her twenties and is now determined that there should be no blame culture at Ann Summers:

'Women have the ability to toughen up but need to go through those difficult experiences first. We have to accept in our careers that, when bad things happen, it is an opportunity to learn. We might think: "This is awful, I can't deal with it," but if a woman sticks it out it helps to develop her. I have actually seen women toughening up as they advance in business. I know I am tough when I need to be. I am very focused and don't dislike myself for it. It is a job and it has to be done. There's no way I get a kick from it and I don't dislike myself for it.'

So the rule has to be, unfortunately, that women have to take the blows and not be deflected. Let's make things change. Psychologist and businesswoman Alma Thomas says this on the subject:

'Women tend to lack assertive confidence. In my profession, I felt not only as good as the men but better, and I believe I am. They

don't, of course, but because I did things differently and developed new directions when I worked with athletes – some of the best in the world, I might add – I was not viewed as "proper sports psycho". There is pressure to conform to the male way of doing things and it's very powerful because women still think only about men's opinions.

'One of my clients is an international singing star and she is constantly anxious about conductors and their opinions and comments. She feels they have power over her and she is always feeling put down. This, from a woman at the very top of the tree. Men are often condescending, offering platitudes and all of that nonsense that women don't like but don't have the guts to say so. Or maybe it's that they don't have the skills to say so. I regularly come across women who don't have the skills to be assertive and so they become aggressive and lose their equilibrium. There are the rare ones who say: "I'll show him."

'Perhaps I am putting women's tendency to lack confidence too firmly at men's door and perhaps it should be at society's door. Men do create the atmosphere to an extent, but many women are very good at falling into the "I must be tall and thin" syndrome, instead of being what they are. That's the crucial point: it is okay to be you. A lot of women wouldn't be able to tell you who they are, but successful women can.'

I have to say I am fortunate because I am not an emotional person and I don't make emotional decisions, so I am confident in why and how I have made my decisions.

Kate Hartigan – managing director of Ina, a Birmingham-based bearings factory with a £100m turnover – also provides useful examples of how confidence can be lost and how it can be regained, and garnishes them with some clearly thought-out advice:

'At primary school I was involved in a bullying incident that shook my confidence for some time. I was slapped about a bit by kids from

another school and I couldn't see why. I didn't know them and it seemed so irrational, and it was just such a shock that anyone should wish me harm, but the memory has stayed with me when other things have long passed me by. It was the first time I realized that persuasion didn't always work and that life was not a bed of roses.

'There is a problem with people who don't possess self-confidence, because they react by showing the less attractive traits, being aggressive and almost bullying to try to hide their own inadequacies. Such people are very hard to work for. I would say that if you are under-confident you must learn to know what you want to do and to know you are good at it, and stick in that area. People will recognize your competence and you can gain further confidence from that.

'Another thing is not to be afraid of finding someone who will be a mentor to you. A lot of good companies allocate mentors to staff but they should not be forced onto people, because they can be uncomfortable as well as useful. The mentor has to be someone who is honest, not unnaturally biased and knows how you are at work. The uncomfortable time comes when he or she says no, and it might be because you are not very good.

'Often there are quicker methods of gaining confidence. Because of my position, I have always had credit control people reporting to me. One woman middle manager was very good at her actual work but did not know how to negotiate with people who were aggressive about not paying. She complained that she felt inadequate. I said to her that the next time it happened to imagine the person had no clothes on. If someone made her feel small she was to think about him or her naked. She laughed and she did it. She had been distracted from her feelings. Within a year she had been promoted to the financial director's personal assistant. She just needed that little trigger and once she got past that point she was well on the way to winning the battle. Perhaps she imagined he was small! I suppose this is assertiveness, which is good if you are not allowing yourself to be browbeaten, but it's easy to try to be assertive and end up by being bloody-minded. You should try to accept other people's *arguments and if you are confident you will find yourself saying to someone: "You're right. I haven't thought about it that way."'*

Here's the last word, from Martha Lane Fox. It is directed at young women:

'Everything comes back to confidence. There is no reason why a woman can't achieve as much as a man, if not more. But she will have her confidence knocked all the time. It isn't fair and it is not right that this should happen to a young woman but it does, all the time, sometimes because she is a woman. Don't be put off. When you are rebuffed, ask again. If you are not being given the same opportunities as a male counterpart, ask for them. If you want to go in a different direction, ask to do so.'

Fear of failure: use your mistakes as signposts to success

We have to learn by experience that failure in one respect or another, often the cause of a loss of confidence, is not fatal. Indeed, as Dame Marjorie Scardino points out, it can be a turning point. She says the sale of her collapsing business was the basis upon which the Economist group appointed her as an expert in acquisitions. Dame Marjorie used a chastening time as a tool to build, not to demolish. Most of all, she rejected worrying about the past and tackled business from another direction.

You will find similar episodes in all our careers. What people think of me doesn't bother me generally, and life in business would be impossible if you did. You need a fair degree of tunnel vision. I have met temporary defeats and felt like packing it in, but I don't; I try to think of them as useful lessons and battle on. This disregard for failure prevents me from being any kind of worrier. I have a philosophy: I ask myself: 'What is the worst thing that can happen if I make this decision?' whether it is private, business or personal. I think hard about it and if I can live with the worst thing then I accept the challenge, and if I can't, I don't.

Jacqueline Gold tells me she has a practical way of preventing worry that will disturb sleep and, if unchecked, wreck those other dreams, the dreams of success. She has a writing pad on her bedside table and, if she wakes up in the night and can't sleep, she writes down what is worrying her, ready to be dealt with in the morning. She says:

'It works, too. I used to stress out badly but now I handle pressure well. I also learned to delegate jobs instead of trying to handle them myself. You know, sometimes you can grow frightened of your own shadow. However, when you realize you are the best at what you do, you see problems as opportunities. One other thing: don't hang on to a lost cause. Let it go and move on to the next item.'

Fear of failure is looked at from another angle by Alma Thomas, who says:

'Business is about being competitive. The thinking is: "If I can't be the best, forget it." That's a hard thing to live up to because you are on a tough road and you have to stand up and compete – you against the others. You will be measured and you will be account- able and you have to be prepared for failure.

'Working with a lot of famous people, I find they have learned to fail and get on with the next thing. They get more things right than wrong, of course, but they accept that they can fail. Now this is a thing a lot of women find hard to do, but they have to realize that it's okay to fail, instead of backing down forever as too many of them do. One of the classic exercises is to ask a person to write down where they have succeeded and where they think they have failed and then tear off the failure bit and throw it away. It is saying more than forget the misses, it is saying remember the hits.

'We are back to confidence here. I say: "I've been there and I messed it up, big time," but they have seen me as a role model and the thought that I made huge mistakes is amazing to them. The suc- cessful person has to go on because she has to go on. I was trained in cognitive therapy and I teach my clients that the action follows

the thought, so if you are thinking in a particular way, you will get that action. If you feel knackered, you will be. If you say: "I can't do that," you won't be able to.

'Teaching people about awareness of what someone is saying to herself and the consequent action is a key element of being successful. Simply, it is: change your thinking, change your life. You know you can do it; you are having a tough time, but you know you can do it. Successful people don't leave it alone; the determination and drive to do the next thing is great in people who are successful.'

Kate Hartigan reflects Alma's view and is just as positive. She says:

'There are fewer women, so we stand a good deal more chance of being noticed when we are successful or when we are not. This cuts both ways, however. You must really believe in yourself, that's the most important thing. Never let it cross your mind that you can't do it and never allow yourself to believe you might fail, because anyone might fail.

'But this visibility of women creates more of a fear of failure. We have to try to learn by our mistakes and it is important that we ask people who have experience for their help. Because women perceive that they have to be better than men to succeed, they sometimes struggle on alone. It is true that a problem shared is a problem halved. It goes further even than this, I think. Asking for advice often leads to a good working relationship, bonding with people around you. You feel supported and, if you are supportive as well, people are only too happy to give in return.

'The value of this is huge. If you tend to deal with things by yourself and blank people out, then life can become unpleasant. I agree with you, Karren, that when you make a mistake you can think almost that life is going to end, and then, in a few weeks' time, you can't even remember details of the problem. Next time one arises, you can look back on that. It helps a lot. I remember one bit of silliness. Budgeting can be an aggressive affair in many companies and I was accompanying a chief executive to our French head office for a budget meeting, having prepared stuff on various projects.*

They had all been priced and copied. Then, the night before the meeting, I woke up thinking clearly that I had misinterpreted a big chunk and the outcome was wrong. I got up, rewrote my copy and then informed the chief executive and altered all the other copies. No one noticed the alterations and then, weirdly, a few days later I thought I might have had it the right way round first time. Normally, if you are hit for six like that, it's for external reasons.'

Control freakery: a problem a lot of women have to control

And what a problem this can be. Maybe it stems from the maternal instinct but one of the besetting drawbacks of being a woman in control is that she wants to be in control of everything within sight. Delegation is the answer, but everyone knows that. Doing it is harder. When she set up in corporate video production, Tina Blake had a lengthy and serious attack of control freakery. Outside her office she directed freelances. Inside, well, let her take up the story:

'It was a year before I employed my first person, a secretary, and in the end I had six full-timers: one did videos, she was my former secretary; then there was reception, telephone sales and two guys on graphics and the web. I must say I was a bit of a harridan because I hate to see people who are not busy. God help them if I walked in in the morning and they were having a chat; I stopped that. Time was money. I'm not saying we didn't have great times, probably because they realized what I was like and actually they all stayed with me. On the other hand it's true to say that there was the potential for having a lot more fun, but in my mind not working meant not getting value for money. I had no patience; it was rush hour all the time. I just would not stop working and in my first year had five days off in 365. I should always have had more staff, but I was a control freak and had to do it myself.

'As time went by I did improve, but my idea of going to work is working. I never liked it when it was quiet and I preferred it when I was busy 14 hours non-stop. I even had extra phones installed so

any caller could come through on another line. I gave each girl two phones, one for dialling out on cable because it was cheaper and the other for incoming calls. Now I realize it was silly, but the reasoning was that a customer might not ring back if the line was repeatedly engaged. I used to say that ours was a service industry and people didn't like answering machines. I still believe it, too. People like a friendly voice on the phone and when I ring up and get an automatic answering system, it takes no time at all for me to be hurling stuff. Nothing in life annoys me more, and I think the only time I lost a job to a competitor was when I told a prospective client that his automatic answering system was useless.'

Jacqueline Gold admits she has a perfectionist's nature, which she thinks can cause paralysis. It is also the source of much success. Alma Thomas thinks women in power tend to want control everything around them:

'In other words,' she says, 'these women are afraid other people think they can't control and aren't in control, and so they try to keep hold of everything. We learn that a good leader can, and must, delegate – and we find that it works. The control issue is a great divider between women who are highly successful at work and those who aren't. Women are inclined to care about what other people think – from the next-door neighbour to a junior staff member – and, rather than risk having no control, seek too much of it. Men just get on with the job and the rest be damned. A woman would do almost anything to protect what she sees as her reputation. There's a great comment along the lines that every woman who has become a premier has been dictatorial. It means, I suggest, that women have to "out-male" the men and if you think about Margaret Thatcher, that would be about right. There must have been an enormous number of skills she wasn't using, and I'm pleased to say that we seem to be moving away from trying to out-male men.'

Delegation: you have to do it for your own good

So you hold all the reins and you begin to discover it can't be this way forever: that you have to put trust in others, not least because, as the clever Dawn Airey says, employing people better than you makes you look better. Being a Mother Hen is truly hopeless. When your business begins to grow, it is impossible: first, to do everything yourself; second, to know everything yourself; and, third, to inspire people to do a good job if they suspect you don't trust them to. Jacqueline Gold has taken a careful look at delegation and says:

> *'There are two reasons why some people don't delegate. They truly believe that they are the only one who can do the job. I was one of those people years ago. I became a workaholic and the only way I could get out of that trap was by delegating. Then you begin to realize that if you don't delegate, not only do you stagnate but you are also not challenging your people. That stops them developing and actually holds them back. So I think that is one problem, one which, if you are a perfectionist, and many women are, will bring you down that path. Stop yourself doing it. The other reason people don't delegate, and I think this is more a male trait, is if you don't feel secure in your own position. When this happens you bog yourself down with so many responsibilities so it doesn't feel to you that you are losing control or that someone will do it better than you can. People who tend to do this will also recruit people beneath them in ability, people who are probably not up to the job, and therefore give them a sense of security.'*

Alma Thomas describes delegation as one of the great skills of management. This is not only because the manager is putting trust in others but because she trusts herself to make judgments about the strengths of other people.

Taking risks: measure the chances but don't be afraid

There are a number of types of boldness in businesswomen, and it is my experience that many of them are much more comfortable when they are taking risks in exploiting ideas or skills than in matters of finance. To begin with, they hate waste, which generally is a big attribute. Sometimes, though, looking after the pennies clashes with risking the pounds, a fact which probably explains why so few women gamble big sums in casinos or on the horses. We like a flutter but not a flier. Men are far more likely to sell the house and car on a business idea. Tina Blake loves the buzz of business, the competition, completing the job, getting paid – everything but financial risk:

> *'I am poles apart from my husband in this. The risk doesn't bother him, he'll just dive ahead with an idea and think about the finance as he goes along. Mind you, he's excellent at finding sources of it. Me? When I set up my video company I wouldn't buy my own equipment for some while because I would have had to update it constantly and if there was no work I wouldn't have been able to make the payments. I'd have made a much bigger profit if I had, but I preferred to pay rent for facilities and make less money. I was good at managing and bringing in business, however, and it's my boast that I never had a bad payment or wasn't paid.'*

Most of us have experienced the moment before we take the plunge. There are those people who welcome such moments because they lead to other things, which is half the trick in business risks. Alma Thomas has the support of considerable research when she says that to be an outstanding performer at anything you have to be a risk taker:

> *'It is one of the features of successful business people. When I abandoned university life to set up a private practice, I took what seemed to many people to be a risk, but I have never regretted it because it has provided me with an interesting, exciting new career. I don't know why women don't take risks in terms of money, although I*

might suggest that there are plenty of us who do take them. Perhaps they might just back away from anything that is too risky – go part-way but not step over the edge.

'But there's not much doubt that you must have a commitment to risk. Those who have it learn that, even if the risk doesn't come off, it's not too bad; better than indecision I would say. They have proved themselves confident enough to make their own choice. It's true that the average woman would find it more difficult to risk house and home on something, but even then, successful ones might well do it. I would, whereas, in our case, my husband David wouldn't, ever. I would remortgage and be up and running, whereas he would be scared of possible repercussions.

'There is a big issue about what is seen to be a male role and for many women it doesn't imply they couldn't do it; it just means that most don't. The role and habit are genetic. About ten years ago I conducted a whole series of conferences about self-development leading to better performances for women in athletics and indus-try, but I have to say I don't think we are getting better. Women I worked with then and women now are fighting just as hard to do those things they want to do. Society is more open now but women aren't feeling any easier and certainly not in my business which is male-oriented and chauvinistic.'

Sacrifices: you will get nowhere without missing out sometimes

There is no point in pretending otherwise. To be successful at all, sac-rifices have to be made. In business, those sacrifices are immense and have claimed victims in droves. We all have friends who have started up on their own and been forced to give up, maybe by finance, maybe by poor planning, all sorts of reasons, but often, when they are really honest with themselves, it is because they felt they had lost more in the social world than they had gained in any other way. Boyfriends fall by the wayside when they realize they are not first priority; the chance to have a family may be lost or delayed (I shall deal with this in another chapter);

friends stop calling so often when you keep having to turn them down; there's no time to play tennis four times a week or go clubbing very often; and there's mum worrying herself to death that you are spending your youth without having enough fun.

All of this may be true but if you have the inclination to succeed, it has to be laughed off as immaterial. Seriously, there is no thrill like making something tick, at least not to those of us who realize there is much more to life than partying. Yes, of course, we love good clothes and dining out and dancing and romance, but they have to be fitted in – they are not priorities. It would be hypocritical of me to say that the rewards in terms of wealth and possessions are not important to us, but they aren't even close to the full reason for our relentless pursuit of business achievement.

When I asked Martha Lane Fox what she enjoyed most about being rich she was puzzled, and finally answered that her shares at some point might be worth millions and she might be able to sell them at some time in the future. She is paid about £130,000 a year and, while that might seem like a lot of money for a 30-year-old, she says:

> 'I know it is half of what I could earn if we were really looking at it properly, but that is not why you do it. I honestly don't believe business people do it for that reason. I don't think people start a business for the money. I live in the same flat I've lived in since I was at Spectrum. I have a Beetle! Yes, my lifestyle has changed, in that this weekend I am going to Sardinia, and I would never normally have been able to fly at the front of the plane, and I am staying in a nice hotel, but it is not the most expensive hotel – that is not my background or my style. I have never been flashy in my upbringing. What has been amazing is being able to take out 30 friends for one of my friends' birthday and surprise them all with a dinner, and that, to me, is preferable to being able to fly to New York on Concorde. So there are some things that are just magic to be able to offer people, but in my daily life I am in the office most of the time; I don't have time to go shopping, let alone spend my money! I am not interested in cars, though I do like shoes!'

We'll all say amen to that! Sly Bailey is uncompromising about the need for hard work and the sacrifices this entails:

'No matter how much hard work you think there might be, there will always be more. Don't ever underestimate how much you have to do. I worked very hard when I was appointed to the board at IPC, some long hours. When everyone else was in the pub, I was working. I didn't feel I was missing out – you have to make choices and if you are not prepared or happy to work hard then you have to think precisely about what you want in life. It is about trusting your instincts because no one else can tell you what is right for you; listening to your own head in terms of what you can do and what makes you comfortable. I find the more you put in, the more you get back – and then amazing things happen to you.'

Education: learning isn't necessarily about going to university

University education may be desirable in a businesswoman but it is a long way from being essential. Indeed, the number of non-university educated women, including myself, who run or own companies is surprisingly high. Like me, Sly Bailey responded to on-the-job training and so did Anne Wood, Jacqueline Gold, Kate Hartigan and several others. Sly was 22 before she even began to guess at her potential; Anne was 50 before she was persuaded to form her own production company; and Jacqueline and I accepted chances to manage and create business in our early twenties. I have no idea how our careers would have differed had we taken our educational opportunities, but I am inclined to think we would have done no better than we have.

You don't have to be a Mensa member to understand that certain business practices have to be adhered to – in particular, that you should always know financially where you are and where you are intending to go. There are many traps, and my advice to anyone making her way in business is that she needs a mentor and confidant. At St Agnes convent grammar school in Birmingham, Kate Hartigan considered a variety of careers. She went through her wanting-to-be-a-vet stage, she hated science and she didn't like the idea of law, medicine or education, but thought 'the mysterious world of business sounded interesting.' She wrote to universities, hoping to study business with German, and then a relation suggested she should try to persuade the West Midlands Gas Board to sponsor her and, although she was told the company didn't do that, it did provide professional courses.

Later, for a while, she was to regret that she hadn't been to university, for CV purposes at least, but three years' training in the gas industry undoubtedly provided her with a running start. 'This wasn't business training as such,' she says, 'so my first professional qualification was secretarial and administration. Halfway through I realized I enjoyed accountancy. I am good with logic and numbers, and patterns and balance appealed to me. Three job moves along the way, Kate used the time when her baby was small and she worked in the mornings so she could complete a master's degree. Within days of her full return to work, she was made finance director and her degree no doubt was a further assurance to future employers of her competence.

Conduct: make eye contact but be careful about any other

It is possible, I am told, to sleep your way to the top in films, and probably somewhere near the top in pop music and the lighter forms of theatre. I am certain it is possible to sleep your way to millions by finding a rich and susceptible mate, and there are even cases of the femme fatale becoming an excellent businesswoman of the 'I'm the boss's wife' variety. If you don't or can't or won't choose these options, then the only way to go a long way upwards is through hard work and merit.

On the other hand, I can't see a single reason why a woman should not use her femininity to win friends and influence customers. I would go so far as to say that if she has the spark it is her duty to use it in her own favour. Alma Thomas agrees:

'From personal experience, I am not a good flirt, but I could sell ice to Eskimos. That's because I learned the skills of selling. Interpersonal skills can verge on flirting because I would make eye contact and my style would echo the body language of the customer, making him feel the most important person on earth at time. If that's flirting, fine, but I prefer to think it's having the knowledge of product selling. In selling yourself as a person, you are doing that. Having the knowledge and skills, it would be wrong not to acknowledge that it helps if you look good and companionable. I'll run with that.

'Do I use it? You bet your bottom dollar I do, because it gives me advantage. There are further steps women might take. I'm not sure being one of the lads helps very much. Drinking pints and swearing may help climb a little bit of the ladder, but not much. I wouldn't recommend it. I have been asked a number of times by women performers whether sleeping with the director would improve their chances. My answer is always the same: "It's your choice." But then I talk about attitudes and values. They do not have to do it.'

Kate Hartigan makes an excellent point about humour being a wonderful way of making and keeping relationships, a soother and a bond at the same time, but first she talks about femininity:

'There is so much baggage with the word. A number of my colleagues in other countries shake hands and kiss each other on the cheek as a recognition of a good relationship, especially in Germany. It's almost like a family thing. You have to be careful it isn't too overt because you don't want them thinking the wrong thing. I remember being told that on one job for which I was recruited a very attractive woman was shortlisted and constantly made innuendoes at her interview. Some of the panel were pretty macho and were quite flattered but in the end they all found it too much.

'Now I think humour has enormous qualities in this kind of situation, and throughout business for that matter. I'd go so far as to say it's critical, especially as many of your colleagues will think that women take themselves too seriously. If, halfway through a board meeting, someone quotes from Blackadder, as they do in mine, I *think that's great – it's about the camaraderie, about being in the club. I realized that having good working relationships – laughing with men who were very sceptical of me when I was a young woman doing my first projects – was all-important. You will have disagreements – those are inevitable – but they will be overcome because you respect and support one another. Don't take yourself too seriously. Laughter breaks down barriers. I have found the Germans love an English joke. You may have to explain the humour at first but then they're soon on the wavelength.'*

Key lessons

- *Work on developing your assertive confidence. It will stand you in good stead throughout your working career – and beyond.*
- *We all know to learn from our failures, but don't forget to take confidence from your successes.*
- *You may want to do it all when you start out, but remember, delegating some of your workload to good people will keep you sane and give you more time to do the things that will really make a difference.*
- *Adopt a healthy attitude to risk. You must know your limits, but nothing is ever achieved by being over-cautious*

creating the right culture

This chapter comes with a welfare warning: if you don't like a big workload, read only the next sentence. You should prepare yourself for failure. That said, hard work is as enjoyable as you want it to be. You must never regard it as a chore and only in your weakest moments, perhaps when you unwind at the end of a particularly wearing spell, should you regard it as anything but normal. Always keep in mind your goals and look back occasionally to see just how far you have come – that can be enormously encouraging.

My recommendation is that to stay fresh you must have the occasional break or change of scenery. I don't go along with the theory that a busy woman needs a complete holiday away from everything. That might work for a weekend but I need to stay in touch and I take my mobile phone and, even more useful, my laptop computer with me wherever I go. It doesn't mean I go searching for things to do, because even on holiday I have more than enough to do looking after the family, but I like to be available in anything like an emergency. I'm a busybody and I want to know what is going on in my business. My football club ticks along without me when I'm on holiday for a week. The trouble is, I only half tick along without it. So that's my confession.

The single observation common to every woman in this book is that they have had to work damned hard to be where they are. There are no dissenters from the view that it is the innate genius of women to be able to manage by inclusion – to involve those around them and to try to reach conclusions collectively. Some men manage in this way too, and a few misguided women don't, but whereas men who manage aggressively do rise to the very top, I can't think of a woman who has by being aggressive. When her mind is made up, a woman can be just as tough as the most militant man, but she rarely lets it be seen that way, as her single-mindedness is leavened by understanding. So there we have the two topics of this chapter: hard work and management style. We also cover a related subject: how to deal with the toughest decisions.

Emma Savage is 28 and gave up playing county tennis for Warwickshire because there just wasn't the time to do it as well as single-handedly running her manufacturing business in Halesowen, West Midlands. She said: 'Working until 8.00, 9.00 and 10.00 at night has caused all kinds of problems with boyfriends. Two relationships broke down, one of them a bit because I was out late with contacts. I am completely shattered by the end of the week and I think I've had five days off in the last year. Why do I do it? Well, I suppose it's the buzz – things like when an order is completed and it's loaded and on its way. I just love doing what I do.'

Just how important is hard work?

Emma employs about a dozen men and deals with them directly. They appreciate that she can do every job in her factory. Others in this book employ hundreds, even thousands. Kate Hartigan is also in manufacturing and – unlike Emma, who bravely took over her father's struggling business when he died three years ago – rose by promotion and then by changing jobs. In her way, she has to be just as unsentimental as Emma, most of whose staff come and go. Kate, like Dame Marjorie Scardino, thinks women and men differ very little in their attitudes to inclusiveness, but others disagree. So here in a form of debate are the opinions of Kate, Martha Lane Fox, Jacqueline Gold and Dianne Thompson, with a brief intercession from Sly Bailey. I'm in the chair.

Karren*: Talk of just hard work could put off a woman who wants to go into business. But it has to be faced. Dianne, will you take us through your work processes and how they relate to staff?*

Dianne: No getting away from it that hard work is probably the most important attribute, and anyone who rises to the top without working very hard is very fortunate. However, I think that if you are seen to work hard you do tend to get a response from your colleagues.

You must also be honest and if you come from a background like marketing, as I do, it is very easy for people to bullshit their way through. But you always get caught out in the end, though, and it's far better to say: 'Sorry, don't know but I will find the answer.' People who are not self-confident feel that it is wrong to say: 'Sorry, don't know.' On the contrary, it is a great sign of maturity and people respect you much more if you admit it and come back with a solution.

The third thing I would say is that none of us likes criticism, but if you note it you will find what your weaknesses are and you can work on them. That's really positive. We do 360-degree feedback sessions at Camelot twice a year, and even at my level I forget some of the basics. When I rush into the office, if I am not careful I can go straight in to see my PA, collect my pack and rush out again, not thinking that people might construe this as 'She's in a bad mood today', when actually I am just rather focused.

At my age it is good to have people pull you up at times and make you think about how you impact on them. Camelot employs 900 people, with two large call centres, but we are small enough to be able to communicate easily. We have developed a thing called a verbal cascade, which happens every Monday. It is a team meeting from 10.00 till 11.00 with the execs and then we go out and meet other people, who cascade down as well, so we can guarantee that by lunchtime the whole company has been briefed. It is important to us in a business with a high media profile that we try to make sure our people hear news from us rather than from the media, which is awful.

Karren: Kate, what kind of working environment do you try to create?

Kate: As you mentioned, I think there is no difference between men and women in our objectives. The difference is their personalities. Some women feel they have to be seen as tough or tougher, or maybe that's how they got to where they are. I can honestly say two of the women I worked for had the most autocratic styles I have come across – they were far more difficult to persuade than ever men have been. Maybe it arose because they felt inside that they had to prove something.

If humanly possible I will always go for encouragement and persuasion. If people have been trained properly and they know what they are doing, then all they need is guidance and pushing forward. It is vital that you respect every person for the contribution they make, and just because they are not on the board or senior executives doesn't mean they are any less valuable. After all, you can't run a company with just a pile of managers. Ideally, I want the company to identify what roles are needed and then fill each with a person who has the skills. Then we have to communicate the processes and procedures required, and finally involve people in strategy.

With all those elements we should have a loyal workforce. If you treat people as halfwits who don't need to understand, that's what you will be landed with. As a board, we tend to operate a shared strategy, identifying key steps to get us to where we want to be. Of course, there will be different styles and different ideas, but in the end we must work in the same direction and apply the five values, which are: commitment, integrity, innovation, respect and passion. I don't expect everyone to do everything well and I know I don't suffer fools gladly. However, everyone makes mistakes and so we take the opportunity to investigate why the mistake was made and to make sure it doesn't happen again. If the same mistake is made a second time, then a change might well be necessary. It's a bad message to everyone if people are getting away with not pulling their weight.

Karren: I know you have strong opinions on the blame culture, Jacqueline. Tell us about them, please.

Jacqueline: I don't believe in a blame culture anyway, so if I make a mistake I am the first one to say I am wrong. I'll say: 'I got that wrong, let's learn from that, let's do it this way,' and I think that if you demonstrate this then those around you will feel equally comfortable in admitting the same. When you have a blame culture people will always be covering their tracks, and that is not a healthy culture to be in. When someone covers her or his tracks you quickly begin to lack confidence in the person because you think that they will go and do it again. This area is very much the boss's responsibility, because if she comes down like a ton of bricks on anyone who slips up, then she has to expect them to duck and dive.

Karren: So, Martha, you are in new technology. Is there anything different in the way you treat your staff?

Martha: I am fairly informal. Don't forget I am 30 – I am so lucky to be doing what I am doing and we wouldn't have got anywhere without other people helping us, and so I sit in an open plan office and I feel that it could just as easily have been someone else who got into this crazy position. Part of my enjoyment is being able to build a company, not with friends because you don't make friends necessarily with the people you work with, but with people you respect and colleagues you like. We have done a lot of acquisitions recently and it is interesting to see other business founders who are older. They don't have our culture and some of them quite get off on the boss element.

Creating an inclusive atmosphere

This is not what excited me or Brent at all and I think that it is incredibly important to us for people at lastminute.com to feel that they can just come to us with an idea and say: 'This is crap,' or whatever. It is part of the personality of the brand. Neither of us is ruthless. We are not trying to rip people off. We are trying to create a business in which everyone has a great time, one which customers enjoy, and where people we do deals with feel as happy as we do about the deals. It is very much how we have always tried to build the business, and this filters through from a tiny piece of corporate governance regulation right though to how we reward our staff.

In the past I have tried to be a one-woman HR department but now we have appointed a team in each country and we have just recruited an HR director for the first time. I want HR to be something aspirational, something that enables the business and does not stop it. We would not have got anywhere if we hadn't taken a lot of risks with a lot of people and rewarded them heavily, some of them very heavily, for the risks they took as well.

Karren: Jacqueline, you have strong opinions. I am sure your type of business can't be as relaxed as Martha's. On the other hand…

Jacqueline: Karren, I cringe at the way some people treat their staff. One of the worst things you can do when you are not happy with what someone is doing is to confront him or her. I know how things can get wound up so tight that in the end the manager goes in for confrontation, but it's utterly wrong. Instead of talking through concerns in a relaxed way and working together, they get frightened to let go. It comes as a big shock to someone who thought they were doing well, suddenly to come face to face with this furious boss. It can end at an employment tribunal, costing a bomb, whereas if it had been dealt with day by day from day one we could have had a very good employee. But people get so worked up that they fall into confrontation.

Women are often better with these situations and are a bit more subtle with relationships. Personally, I am interested in the other person's point of view and if a manager isn't happy with, let's say, a woman's attitude or work or she's coming in late, then it's much better to address the problem by asking: 'What's the matter? Can I help you?' Put the ball back in her court, let her have her say, otherwise she'll feel she isn't being treated fairly.

Karren: *I know you think humour can work wonders in some cases, Kate. Otherwise, how do you deal with confrontation?*

Kate: First of all, humour is a marvellous way of taking the heat out of problems. When you are young and a woman and you are trying to make a point with a bunch of blokes who are very sceptical of you, it's amazing what a few smiles and a bit of laughter can do. Actually, I hate scenes and I'll do almost anything to avoid one. No one performs at her best when she's in a temper and I know I don't. Things always seem to go too far. At the same time, there are issues when you have to fight your own corner and if I really believe in something I find very it very stimulating to take part in high-power persuasion.

Before my first main meeting with the German chief executive, I was warned about a German production manager who was known as a bully and would be there. I had presented investment proposals in a way I was used to and started talking about them when this chap started to pooh-pooh. I had picked a particular machine to buy and I knew my proposals were sound. My reaction to his loud objections was to stand up and battle for them. It came as such a shock to him, he really respected it and from then on he was nice to me. There is an important point here. When you know what you are good at on your own ground, that's the time really to go for it. However, the further you climb the more you find there is very little that is black and white, and I've found that if you are fighting for something that isn't worth it, don't be scared to drop it.

At Ina, people think I am entirely in charge but I am just as much an employee as anyone else. If the main board decided on a strategy, even if it is totally against what I think it should be, I implement it because that is what I am paid to do. If I'm not prepared to do so, I shouldn't draw pay.

Karren: *I think we are unanimous about being inclusive. A few words from Sly and Dianne about what this means to them.*

Sly: People shouldn't be asked to fit in with the way the boss works and that's that. I think she should spend time working with individuals to understand how they operate and why they do it that way. She should try to ensure that the chemistry she is developing with each person is helpful. It is her responsibility to manage it and sometimes to create a distinct relationship with each person. She should be consistent in her expectations of people but she should be prepared to go a bit further to make things work.

Adopting the right management style

Is that a female characteristic? It is like anything else, isn't it? Compare it with your home life, your relationships and the way you are with friends and family. Perhaps those characteristics are not that different in business and you don't need to throw all of them off when you go to work.

Dianne: The story of being a good boss for me is about being honest and being open – that is very important. I have an open-door policy and I encourage anyone who has had a great idea to send it to me, and I get them all the time. Although I have an office, I have got rid of all the others and I am out walking the floor all the time.

Karren: Dianne, I am sure you had some stressful experiences when Richard Branson appeared to be winning the right to replace Camelot as National Lottery organizers. How did your staff respond?

Dianne: Being a woman was an advantage at that time we lost the second licence in 2000. It was Branson with his media image against me, a feisty northerner and, vitally, that's what kept the story alive and helped us to challenge the decision.

My predecessor here as MD was Tim Holly, who was popular because he had created Camelot and won the first licence. There are still a lot of people at Camelot who were there from November 1994 when we launched, and I was worried how I was going to take over from him after he stepped down. We are very different people. Tim was a project manager and actually launching the National Lottery was one of the biggest projects ever. The challenge now is how do we get back into sales growth, so a sales and marketing background is far more appropriate.

I didn't worry about how I was to replace him in their minds because it was natural they felt great affection for him. But the whole drawn-out fight transformed this because there was so much coverage of me in profiles and interviews. Suddenly everyone here knew all about me. Beforehand I'd pass people on the steps and they'd ask how I was and then walk away, but this changed. Instead they would stop me and say things like: 'Hi Di. When does Jo [her daughter] get her GCSE results?' and they really felt they knew me. They had read so much that they felt very passionate that I was out there fighting for their jobs. They did some lovely things. I came back one Friday and there was a bottle of Bollinger on my desk with a note from our helpline staff saying: 'Have a drink from us this weekend.' There were some lovely gestures.

Karren: We have alluded to making tough decisions. I would like to ask the youngest of us here, Martha, whether she thinks women are less able to be strong when the chips are down.

Martha: In some ways women can be much more direct, really straight-forward, but when it's about themselves they find it harder, which is a kind of under-confidence, I think. Would I trust a woman more than a man if I said: 'Go into this meeting and tell this person that they are not performing because of this and that'? I believe women would normally do this five times better than a man. A man would normally dance around it and not necessarily reach a conclusion and feel a bit awkward about the personal conversation, whereas women can be very good about just being clear and straight and slightly sympathetic.

Dealing with the unpleasant side of business life

As a business we are not shy about making acquisitions, but to me that does not mean you get aggressive. One of the worst days of my life at lastminute.com was in November 2002 when we had to make our whole customer services team redundant – 100 people – because we outsourced. These were people who for three or four Christmas periods had ridden their bikes around London to deliver presents for customers. They were like friends and I stood up in front of them and told them what was happening. If I had hidden away or done it aggressively it would have been really bad. But I think I did it the right way. My attitude is that redundancies are just part of business life but that doesn't mean you can't treat people fairly, be completely straight with them.

In the difficult times it is even more important that you are absolutely honourable. It would have been ruthless if I had said: "We are making you redundant", paid them only a week and tried to get away with it. But it was clearly the best thing for the group, and by moving and restructuring the group it made the majority of other people's roles safer, putting the business in a stronger position. We treated every single one of those people with respect and fairness, but ultimately businesses have to opt for survival and generating shareholder value.

Kate: I don't have the dirty work of telling people they no longer have a job, redundancy that is. But we share these decisions as a board and feelings about it are always strong and deep. I don't like scenes; my method has always been to persuade, taking the facts for and against and weighing them in the balance. I can't shout and rave. Most plans of action are collaborative, but you can't run a business by committee. In the boardroom it's my role to ensure that all the pros and cons are listened to, but ultimately I make the decision and I do so based on what I think is the best way forward from my own feelings. Bottom line is that, whether people are for or against a decision, they will do their damnedest to carry it through. In a good team that is what happens. It is my feeling that cold eyes are far more chilling than shouts. There are some people who are quietly ruthless, with the determination to do it their way no matter what anyone else thinks. In this respect I can't say women are more sensitive than men – men may show it differently.

Making people redundant is hard whoever you are; firing is something else. If I have to fire someone, that will usually have been the conclusion of a series of issues. If it is for under-performing, we'll have identified the areas and the person concerned will have been given every opportunity to put things right. Ultimately, then, if we have to part company it's not a big surprise. Redundancy, though, is such a shock to people – they feel they have been stabbed in the back.

Karren: I know Jacqueline was involved in a fascinating story that shows the kind of strong mental attitude women must have when they reach high executive status. 'No nonsense' describes it well, I think. Jackie?

Jacqueline: I believe women find it easier to deal with people in a straightforward way and we do have the ability to toughen up, although perhaps we need to go through difficult experiences first. A lot of men do, too, of course.

First, we have to accept that when bad things happen in our careers, they are opportunities to learn. You might think: 'This is awful. I can't deal with it,' but these experiences help you develop and so you have to stick them out. I actually see women toughening up; I felt myself toughening up, after all. I try only to be tough when I need to be, but I am extremely focused and I don't dislike myself for doing my job as I think fit – but I certainly don't get a kick out of it. In the end, it's just a job and it has to be done.

I have a perfect example in my father and his problems with having to sack someone. He had a chief executive, very senior, who started by doing a very good job but then saw himself as powerful, so powerful he even appointed himself chairman of one of the companies. The atmosphere was untenable and soon this man was not bothering to call board meetings. It became so bad my father couldn't bear to be in the same room as he was. He was so autocratic he intimidated people to such a degree that the staff were frightened. My father just delayed and delayed. It's a family tradition that dad, my sister and I go out once a week to chat and enjoy ourselves, relaxing with the people we know best. It reached the position where this man was dominating conversation. We agreed he had to go but dad still wouldn't do it. Finally, I started to communicate with him and sent him a letter saying I wanted to meet him at a specific hotel. This set a point of no return. I went to the hotel by myself and explained to him that things weren't working out in the way we wished. He obviously realized this and he left the company.

I know my father couldn't have done that and in my experience I think men find it harder to enact this kind of decision. My MD at Ann Summers, also a woman, uses the needs of the business as her focal point and strength. Generally, it's the woman of the family who will go and talk to the headmaster in her child's interests. And it's me, not my partner, who goes to see the neighbours if there's an issue. Women aren't aggressive in the way men tend to be. Again, my partner finds it easier to deal with a confrontation or issue by going in aggressively. He'll often say he wishes he could be more diplomatic.

Karren: *So explain your philosophy with staff, Jacqueline. I think it is enlightened.*

Jacqueline: It's much better to talk to the other person and win them around. People will compromise if they believe you understand and appreciate their position. We all have confrontations in our lives, they are inevitable, but if you get yourself heated or allow your temper to rise, perhaps to the level of the person you are dealing with, the stress is enormous. I deal with the situation calmly. I am very organized and I plan beforehand, thinking things right through. Maybe I take ten minutes on it now but in my twenties I might have thought about it all day. You must insist to yourself that this isn't a confrontation, and go in thinking that.

I do try to consider it from the other person's point of view, and you can often use this to your advantage. Having sympathy with a view or cause wouldn't stop me dealing with it. If I have to make people redundant, I'll do it with compassion, but it won't stop me doing it. If I find someone cheating, I'll get rid of the cheat as cleanly as possible without being ruthless.

A place for compassion

In this business we have quite a few debtors. We chase the debt and if it's not paid we hand the whole matter to a debt collecting agency. If someone has personal problems, we try to act with compassion, but eventually it might be necessary to hand over to someone for an independent judgment.

My guiding principle is that everyone in the business should be treated equally. And I hate things to fester. In one case a poor relationship was developing between two executives, a man and a woman, and I insisted they had to talk it through. It had to be clear to them that they had to focus on the business first, refuse to become involved in emotional issues and overcome their antipathy to each other.

Because you are the boss, people put you on a pedestal and are intimidated. My door is open all the while because being approachable is very important to me and to the business. Conscious of not appearing aloof, I like to give people a welcoming smile and be warm towards them. In meetings, I try to get everyone's opinion on the table because I am sure it is only in this way that you get the best from them. It's easy to become so busy and so stressed that you dismiss people's ideas and opinions without real thought. We do all kinds of things, fun days and barbeques to promote loyalty and friendship. We recognize loyalty and achievement by presenting prizes, and we like partners and colleagues to be there to share in success – that can be very inspirational to people. Then we have think-tank meetings, monthly meetings with different staff telling us how they think we can improve and they can improve. A huge number of ideas come in. A lot of companies drift into the position where staff are in the dark and they begin to lose trust to the extent that they refuse to believe a new initiative will help them, even if it would. It's a simple thing to keep staff informed but you'd be amazed how many companies don't.

When Ann Summers moved a mile up the road to a new building, it ought to have made people feel happy, but instead it made them nervous, nervous about moving. For some, turning a desk round is the big issue of the day, so we had some very tender nerves to deal with there. We kept everyone informed all the time, department by department, and when they arrived at our new home there was a box of chocolates for everyone, a pack describing the new building and its facilities, and we added that we hoped they would all be happy there, and welcome and thanks for their hard work. There was no real cost to us and we recognized that they were all part of the family.

Karren: *A final word from Dianne on the subject of women in charge.*

Dianne: I believe women serve their companies better than men do, because they believe in them and know that they are there to do a job, whereas some men seem to be there only to serve themselves. A woman would be loyal to the company, serve it and make the decisions not for herself but purely for what is right for the company.

There is a second thing: women are natural nurturers of people and will bring people on and encourage them. If a woman thinks she is employing someone who could do well but who isn't fulfilling herself in a particular job, she might well try to encourage her or move her to where she succeeds, and give her part of the credit. A lot of men are 'My way or no way.'

I care about my people and I know a lot about them and their families. It is all part of being a team, but I am decisive and I see my role where I try to set the direction and the rest of the team decide the best way to get there. Occasionally there are some very tough decisions to be made, like last year when we felt we had to make 88 people redundant.

Karren: *Those, I am sure, are the worst times. The best? When all that hard work, all that caring management sets the scene for, as we say in football, a result!*

Key lessons

- *Never underestimate the value of hard work in getting your business plans off the ground.*
- *Business life can be uncompromising and full of tough decisions that need to be made, but always be sure to use tact, diplomacy and compassion wherever possible.*

family ties

This book strongly asserts that a woman can have children and continue to be successful in business, just as she can take leave for a while before returning to contribute with as much effect as ever. The first option is the more testing, I am in no doubt about that, but I have two young children, so I know it can be done. I am not going to be euphemistic and I am certainly not going to brag about this. Nevertheless, having a family and working full-time on a career that can never be 9 to 5 is challenging, complicated and wearing; sometimes remorselessly tiring. Never, ever, imagine otherwise.

Increasingly, subsequent modern generations of women will reject having children in favour of career choices and, perhaps as they see it, more fun, fewer ties and no nappies. But then they are missing something that to me is even more fulfilling than success in business or the finest clothes or the best shopping. I always intended to have children and now I have two, Sophia and Paolo. They are our jewels, utterly separate from my life of work, although I admit that when I drive in to do something out of hours, Sophia loves to come with me and sit outside my office, completely preoccupied in her world of drawing, painting and designing. Without them, part of my life would be empty, but I am not emotional about this. My husband Paul and I made a choice and we have never for a second regretted it.

If you decide against having children, that can only be your own affair and, goodness me, there are plenty of reasons why a career woman might believe that children are a lifestyle she can do without. Anne Wood did not even found her business until her two children had grown up; Dame Marjorie Scardino has three; Kate Hartigan one; Dianne Thompson one – so it is perfectly possible to obtain a balance between family life and high achievement, even if it can be precarious. Dianne, like me, admits to anxieties and tensions, whilst Kate appears to have organized her motherhood with barely an instance of the milk boiling over. I am sure she had moments of stress, but overall hers was a plan that succeeded marvellously. In 1983, when she became pregnant, she was employed as working capital controller by Alcad Ltd in Worcestershire, a subsidiary of an American company making batteries. Let her expand:

> '*I was about 30 and my husband and I both wanted a child. We had spoken vaguely about it but only as a future thing. I had been with the company three or four years and it was time to either move on or stay and get pregnant. I had a quiet word with the financial director, explaining that I didn't want to come back quickly full-time but I would be prepared to do mornings. I knew I could do the job in that time but I wouldn't be able to do all the other jobs they had always been keen I should do. When your boss knows you are keen, he tends to use you for all kinds of things. In a couple of years I would return full-time. He said: "Do that. I'd much prefer it to losing you."*
>
> '*I knew when I returned I would have a lot of hours to give back, and after having a baby daughter I began to think what qualifications I needed to stand out for promotion. It was obvious, really, although my friends thought I was insane to do it. Because I hadn't been to university, I decided on a master's degree and got an MA in*

accounting and finance. *It worked out for me because my mother-in-law lives close by and she babysat two mornings a week and I had a friend who child-minded for the other three mornings. Because they both lived nearby, when I did work a bit late – I couldn't always resist that – they would stay over. There's no doubt you have to be able to rely totally on that kind of support.*

'*After two years, Alcad wanted me back full-time, and no sooner had I returned than I was promoted to financial accounts manager, so my CV was back on track. When my daughter was four, I was made financial director, so it all worked out rather well. I don't remember feeling any more tired then than I do now, but I always found work invigorating.*

'*By the time I was 30, I pretty well had partying and that kind of thing out of my system. I suppose I was more of a home body. My husband and I tried to be a unit of three and when, for instance, I played squash, my daughter would come along with me. She wasn't farmed out; she always went with us. I suppose looking after two children would be more than twice as difficult but our marketing manager has two after having six months off each time. But it is true that a mother can be disadvantaged by more or less having to stay in the same job while others may be moving on and up and there is this perception that a mother is always saying: "Sorry, I have to rush off." It's easy to be so busy that you lose friendships too. On the other hand, I started skiing when my daughter was four and took up golf when she was ten, and, honestly, I don't think she missed much that other children had.'*

It would be practically impossible for a mother to continue in business without daytime help. Both she and the children would suffer, and never get anything done. The help may come from a relative, a reliable child minder, an old-fashioned 'nanny' or even a husband. Typically American, Dame Marjorie takes a positive and refreshing view of her family, looked after much of the time by her husband.

'They have made my career possible. Not only have they given me courage and support, but they've also reminded me that I'm never as great or as terrible as the newspapers or the analysts or anyone else I encounter may say. They have kept me focused on the things that matter rather than on the things that other people say matter.

'And, I do subscribe to what may be more truism than fact, that having children helps you learn to do more than one thing at a time – definitely a requirement in business. Of course, the demands of family are thankfully an experience shared by more and more men these days. I don't have any special formula for family life, I never found juggling in a methodical way (Tuesdays are for …) very appealing. I like a little chaos. I'm sure I haven't done a textbook job of juggling family and work, and that my family has taken up a lot of slack. The only advice I can offer is – be clear about which comes first when there's a contest. Feeling that the work I do has meaning is a great help. My family also keeps me honest – mostly by reminding me I'm spending too much time doing things that look boring to them.'

The motherhood experiences of Kate and Dame Marjorie appear so worry-free that it would be misleading of me to leave any reader thinking that she could just have a couple of children, juggle the baby-sitters and enjoy a perfect arrangement. In my case, it can still be more like engaging in a comedy of re-arranged schedules and hurried appointments, not to mention ringing mobile phones. I am not complaining but if you, like Dame Marjorie, enjoy a bit of chaos, you should try two children, a husband who has to train 100 miles away and often absent at football matches, combined with running a Premier League football club. More of this after Dianne has spoken of her years on the tightrope between the demands of love and the obligations of work:

'When I was working at Sandvik my husband and I separated. I was doing an awful lot of overseas travelling with it being a foreign-owned steel company so I needed a job with very little travel as my

daughter was seven years old. In fairness to my president he did say at the time of the separation that my instinct would probably be to move jobs but I shouldn't as the firm were our family now and "we can give you a support system." This was great but it was in Sweden. I needed to move as the travelling was too much and without realizing it they were putting huge demands on the senior people. These were probably more manageable for some of the guys. For example, there used to be 12 overseas board meetings and the rule, a very good one, was that they always started at 9 on the Monday morning of the local time, which meant Sunday flights. It also allowed the board to start on time but cost 12 Sundays out of 52. Then there were other foreign trips.

'So the two of us moved to London, with me as director of marketing at Woolworths for three years. I was headhunted to join Cygnet and, despite all the traumas and pressures I have at Camelot, that was the hardest job I have ever had. We turned it round, but it was very, very hard. During this time I had live-in help for my daughter and I have to say that had my then-husband and I been smart enough to do this when we were married, there may never have been a divorce. We didn't like the idea of having full-time help, but when you are on your own and you are doing business dinners and travelling as well, you need someone.

'Then when Jo was 12, our housekeeper decided she wanted to go back to looking after babies again. Jo and I had another conversation about whether we should try on our own again and that is what we did. There are days when I have a crisis and that was particularly tough when we first moved to London because I did not know a soul and I am an only child. The whole concept of work/life balance is becoming far more important now. At Camelot we have put in some fairly dramatic changes and part of this is because, being a single parent, I understand the pressures so much more. We have job sharing. We have working from home and we have extended hours working where a person might opt to do 7 to 6 four days a week and do a five-day-a-week job in four days, then have a long weekend. We have been very flexible and the only difficulty for me *is that I know I have to be a role model in following this mode and yet I still feel guilty if I leave early one afternoon.*

'Of course the higher someone climbs the more it is a 24-hour job, including late nights and early mornings. I have not had to cancel holidays but I have had to come home early or spend half the holiday on the phone, which upset my daughter. It goes with the territory and I tell her it is a way of life and not a job. I was married young but we didn't have Jo until I was 33 and then I took six months off, so I was well into my career by then. Perhaps if I had had her when I was 23 it might have been different. It is hard but, unlike some people, I have always been able to turn off.'

I was in my mid-twenties when Sophia was born and the event, unfortunately, coincided with the end of the 1996 season. Football club managers are sacked all the time. Each one lives with the probability that sooner or later the chairman or MD is going to call him into his or her office and explain that 'Sorry, the time has come for a parting of the ways.' For public consumption this may be described as a sacking, resignation or mutual parting but, let us put it this way, few of them are surprised at their departure. We are a results business and managers know that bad results equal loss of job. The consequence is as inevitable as frost on geraniums.

I am making this digression because, for anyone who doesn't know about football lore, the fact that I dismissed a manager, Barry Fry, within a week of giving birth to Sophia, may seem ruthless. It wasn't. Probably Barry knew as well as the board that we believed at the time that he had reached the limit of his potential and we still were nowhere near promotion from the First Division. Indeed, we had remained loyal when we were relegated to the third-ranking division for only the second time in our 125-year history. We compensated him well, as befitted a manager who had raised the club profile enormously, and who still evokes great affection from everyone at St Andrew's, myself included. As a board, we are strong on loyalty to managers. Trevor Francis remained with us for five-and-a-half years on the basis of three near misses at promotion. Trevor's appointment was confirmed before Sophia had formed her first smile.

Sophia was born to order, I suppose. I chose a hole in my diary and rang our doctor with the request that I should give birth at that time. I was back at work within a week. I did not realize it at the time but this was the easy bit. We had always planned to have a family and for me to continue to work, but I don't think I ever really calculated on how hard it would be to juggle both roles.

My mother came to help and my mother-in-law came over from Canada and for the first six weeks I had lots of support; after that I took on a nanny. But, though I had help I was at work all day, and up all night with Sophia. Sometimes in the middle of the night I would think: 'I can't do this, both parts of my life are important, but I cannot give 100% to each.' Something had to give. Physically, I was exhausted, people prepare you for all sorts of things when you are expecting a baby, but the one thing you can never prepare for is the constant tiredness. I still suffer with it now.

Managing your time at home

I found out about myself in those early days, found the resilience to carry on. And, being me, having done it once with Sophia, it didn't put me off having another baby, Paolo. At least I knew what to expect and this time around I took off 4 weeks. Sometimes I would think: 'Who has got me where I am?' and answer: 'Me.' This was hugely motivating to me. The one consistent element of my life is my job. I created it. I built it.

Time is the most valuable commodity in the world and you realize it when you have a young family. Then again, I expected the time pressures to ease as the children grew older, but I find there is even less of it now. As babies, they are so precious and fragile but their demands are simple: eating and sleeping mostly. But soon they want and need more attention, and time management becomes an art in itself. Some of the methods are, I think, unique to me, but it has to be this way when you are a working mother. I don't know of anyone else who goes to bed at eight as regularly as I do, with a child tucked up on either side, listening to stories or just chatting about what has happened to us that day. Time management is essential for us all, but to no one more than a woman who is starting a business or beginning to establish it. Only an exceptionally brave woman would have a baby at such a time, because either the baby, her relationships and/or herself would suffer badly. I certainly know that I could not have turned around Birmingham in 1993 if I had a newborn.

I often read about these 'superwomen', working mothers who have it all: top job, plenty of kids and a wonderful relationship. I am not doubting for one second that there are women like this, but my experience from all the working mothers I know is that it is certainly not easy having two roles. All working mothers develop two personalities; the trick is keeping one from draining the life from the other.

Its impossible to be in two places at once; board meeting or nativity play? Now there's a choice.

The one thing we all have in common is that we are always trying to play catch up; making up to the kids for not attending the play or making up to the office for leaving early to attend the play. It's a constant juggle, sometimes you'll drop one of the balls. The key for me is to find your own balance, as you won't be able to do it all, but you can do all the things that are important to you.

The hardest word for us all to say is 'no', whether this be at work or at home. But learn to say it. I say no to 99% of the invites I receive, sometimes to the most wonderful events, premieres and dinners, but I am realistic enough to know that I work all week, and have two kids, I just cannot do it all, and therefore I give these things up.

I don't leave my children overnight unless I absolutely cannot get back home - even if it's 4 a.m., my view is that if I am not there to tuck them in, I will be there when they wake up. I never go on holidays without my kids; if I have time off I spend it with them. I rely on my best friend Suzanne who organizes trips, pick ups and drop offs ... and secretly I wish I had a wife like all my fellow CEOs in football, and then life would be complete!!

I often say that the last thing on my list is always myself and that's just the way it is for working mothers, but recently I worked out that being a mother and having this great job is actually all I need or want from life.

In a budding business it is necessary to develop an operational style, consciously having to plan nearly every minute, and I don't think this would be possible for a young mother. I had to smother the notion of having children for some while. It might be 9.30 in the evening at work and I would suddenly find myself musing about a baby. Then I would tell myself: 'Don't be ridiculous,' and pick up my pen again. To illustrate how squeezed for time I am, a magazine recently sent me an e-mail asking me to supply some time-saving tips for readers. I replied: 'Yes, don't bother answering e-mails like this!'

The impact of a family on your career progression

Not too many employers would argue that there is an advantage in career progression for a woman who chooses not to have a family, and some (confidentially) would admit that the fear of a young woman having a baby might affect her chances of being taken on. In a small business, where a woman having six or nine months' maternity leave could have a notable effect on production, the employer might be very sceptical. Jacqueline Gold says:

> *'It should be no surprise that there are not more successful women in business. I think there are three reasons. The first is that a large percentage of women do choose to go down the family route rather than going to work. Second, sadly, is that there are not sufficient facilities for mothers to return to work. I must admit that at Ann Summers we would love to help more mothers back to work, but we need government help. For us to set up a crèche is really difficult, impossible even. If we had space and all the facilities, we could take only half a dozen children and that wouldn't anywhere near achieve the number to make it viable. And, third, is that there is pressure from partners for women to be at home with them. It is expected of a woman and she is looked on critically if she chooses to have a family and develop her career. It is also true that some male employers will be reluctant, often subconsciously, to help because they think she will decide not to return after having a baby. My company has 7500 organizers and 1000 employees, and I would say 90% are women.*

'We try, first thing, to stay in contact during maternity leave. This helps their confidence and we also give plenty of flexibility about when they return. We have kept many excellent staff by running voucher schemes to assist them to use nurseries. I take the view that it is stupid to invest a lot of money on a person and just let her go. In financial terms, too, we spend £250,000 a year on recruitment, and one way of cutting that cost is to invest in encouraging mothers to return to work. As for actual appointment, if I thought we were recruiting a woman who intended to start a family imminently, it would need thinking through. If I knew she intended to in three or four years' time, and it came to a choice between two people – a man and a woman, maybe – I would take the best-qualified candidate.'*

Like Jacqueline, Martha Lane Fox has no children. She is adamant that sexism is behind the fact that so few women have become major players in business. Time out to have children is, she believes, used by men as an excuse for lack of promotion. She said:

'A talented woman having time away to have a baby shouldn't matter at all. It is just a red herring to me. If a man values having a woman as part of the top team, she should be promoted regardless, and the firm should find ways to work around the time she has to have off. In economic terms, this is absolute common sense. Structurally, this country is still geared in business far more towards men than women, although sometimes women don't help themselves. Some of the issues about lack of confidence and failure to promote their own cause may lead a company to underrate them or not give them sufficient consideration. Women need to overcome these deficiencies if they are going to make the next breakthrough. However, I do believe that if a chief executive really believed it was going to create more value in the company to have a half-male, half-female board, it would happen.'*

Martha does not entirely subscribe to the idea that an executive has to work herself to exhaustion to be successful. I must say I think I am being more realistic in believing that she does have to, unless she is lucky enough to be in an industry that values ideas and initiatives more highly than having the skills to push them through. However, her opinion is valuable:

'I don't buy this thing that you need to be working 24 hours a day, seven days a week, to be brilliant. It is a culture engendered a lot more by men but I think that if you really focus on what people are delivering rather than the hours they are spending, sometimes wastefully, then a shorter week is possible for women who are rigorously organized and pack a lot into their hours.

'You do have to be pretty spectacular to manage a home life and a high-flying working life, but it can be done, even if it means that you can't go out to dinner twice a week. I don't have children so I am not well qualified to say what effect they have, but I am sure it could be managed if you had the money. I am certain, though, that it is worth compromising on hours in order to have outstanding women in the organization and not to worry about the fact they have to go home at five o'clock. The same would apply with maternity leave. Great women are vital to an organization.'

According to Alma Thomas, it takes a certain kind of woman to run a business and a family. She contends that, although this woman will be very involved as a wife, lover and mother, she will always keep a sharp focus on her own identity. That is essential to her. Then Alma goes on to make an intriguing point, one which I deal with more comprehensively elsewhere. She, like Anne Wood and Ricky Rudell, saw business life beginning at 50. It was around that age that each set a new course and became highly successful. Alma said:

'Many women have problems when the children leave home, based on the assumption that their practical life and usefulness is at an

end. Such a woman has not felt the need to assume her own identity and to feel that it's worthwhile to keep a hold on that. Obviously, the women who have always been successful will not have stopped working, but for thousands of others 50 is a wonderful age to start a business. With confidence and self-esteem, it is perfectly possible to catch up on skills and technological developments. I did. I walked out of academic life and that was it. My husband still hasn't recovered from the shock.'

Key lessons

- Having a family on top of a full workload will be demanding and challenging, but ultimately immensely rewarding.
- Family life will give you a focal point, and is also great for keeping the rigours of work firmly in perspective.
- Learn to manage your time effectively, so that you can make the most of precious time spent at home with your family.

the winning habit

The first of my two case study chapters (Chapter 5) concerned women who have been strikingly successful in the media. This, the second, centres on two young women who, in diametrically contrasting businesses, have done exceptionally well but have heights yet to conquer. In one way or another, achievers have to be competitive, although this may not necessarily be in the macho-male, tooth-and-claw form. There are plenty of instances of women being competitive within themselves, generating their drive through the belief that they are capable of doing almost anything they set their minds to.

Although a football stadium is probably the most competitive arena you will find short of the New Year sales, I have to admit I am not sporty and that my competitiveness is of the introvert kind. Emma Savage, 28, and Karen Blackett, 32, were both accomplished sportswomen and admit to the enjoyment of winning, pure and simple. Emma, a Warwickshire county tennis player, gave up the game to concentrate entirely on running the vehicle precision components business she inherited from her father when he died three years ago. Karen, the eye-catching daughter of Bahamian parents who came to this country before she was born, was a useful junior sprinter. Nowadays she keeps gloves and pads in her office at Mediacom, where she is marketing director, so that she can later work off her aggression at kick boxing. She is a black belt. Emma is fair-haired, attractive and carries herself like a sports player. She went to Edgbaston High School, Birmingham, where the custom is to pass on to university well-spoken young ladies with sound qualifications, rather than tomboys in oil-stained overalls to a metal components factory. She left school with nine GCSEs and is glad she did, such was the call of the factory life. Let her take up the story:

'I suppose I was six or seven when my father, Gordon, first took me to his lovely big factory in Blackheath. From the earliest days, I was at home in the environment, a shop full of working machinery turning out metal objects. At 16, I couldn't wait to work full-time and dad backed me. My mother would have preferred me to stay on at school for A-levels at least. For eight years I worked on the shop floor, first at Blackheath and then, after a supermarket chain bought the land, here at Mucklow Hill, Halesowen. There's no job in the building I can't do, from beginning to end, from changing tips to programming the computers, and I would far rather be in the factory than in my office where I spend most of the time these days.

'I was never shocked by the shop floor language, although I have no idea whether they try to curb it when I am around. I suspect not, because these days they are more likely to suffer from mine. No, I have no difficulties being the only woman around working men. I am great pals with one guy here, Ali, the shop foreman, who is priceless to the firm and has worked for my father and me for 26 years. When I'm feeling a bit down or I need help, he's always around and he'll work night and day to get an order done on time.

'From the start I loved the muck, oil and suds. My hands are always getting cut and on one occasion my hand slipped on a grinding machine. It slashed through the tendons to the bone and I nearly lost a finger. I can't stand the sight of blood and I was close to fainting as my hand was bandaged before I was taken to hospital. I had just passed the driving test and I couldn't drive because my hand was in a splint. The boys on the floor were doing impressions of me, so I told them to shut up and get on with work.'

So there was Emma, cursing with the lads on the shop floor, while Karen took a more conventional route, gaining her geography degree at Portsmouth University. She had been a pupil at a comprehensive school and then passed three A-levels at Henley College. Of this time, she says:

'My dad and mum came to this country in 1962 on a British government scheme, she as a nurse and he as a bus conductor, later working for BT. Reading is a mini-Barbados and my sister, Susan, and I had a typical West Indian upbringing. I was always very competitive and by the time I was four I could do the six times table. My parents were quite strict and vocationally focused, wanting us to have a serious education and good jobs and, actually, my sister is an accountant. They made a point that we always had to try twice as hard as anyone else because we were not only black, but we were female. Being average was just not good enough. My geography degree course encompassed a wide range of subjects: criminal psychology, statistics, retailing and any number of other things as well as physical geography. I worked very hard and really enjoyed it but a lot of us on the course were not quite sure what we wanted to do when we left.'

Getting stuck into the challenge

While Emma took up the very physical challenge of factory work, Karen embarked on a more structured course of employment. Actually, like many of us, she set off in her current direction almost by accident, although it might have been fate. During the six months that she was jobless she studied IT and computers on a vocational course. Then she had two interviews with CIA Direct, a small media-buying agency. She was offered a job after her third interview and started work four days later as a novice media planner and buyer. She was quickly caught up in the exciting, pressurized atmosphere:

'I loved it there. It was quite a small operation, about 10–15 people, and the hours were stupid, 9.00 a.m. to 7.30 or 8.00 in the evening,

and every so often to 2.00 a.m. if we were pitching for business. It seemed normal because everyone was doing it. I had two female bosses in succession and they became close friends. We really were all in it together. Then I made a mistake: I moved.

'I was 23 and I had the feeling that I was too comfortable with everyone and I had stayed at CIA for too long. I went to a much bigger agency, Zenith, chiefly because I had enormous respect for the media strategist there. However, I discovered that the things that had inspired me to join his company didn't exist. It was entirely the wrong agency for me and now I know that you should never move because of one person and you should never try to stick things out. I didn't. I left after only five months to join Media Business and I got that one absolutely right.

'I was wrong to move to Zenith but there was nothing wrong with taking the risk. You have to be brave and put yourself on the line because fear of failure can be crippling. But once you realize a thing is wrong, move away quickly. One senior woman at Zenith asked how on earth I could leave a big, successful agency for a corner-shop version, my decision was considered so bizarre. But once Media headhunted me and I had talked to three directors about the culture, I was always going there. Zenith did not encourage individuality, it tried to turn out clones, process-driven and formulaic. I like room to experiment. At Media Business, there was a degree of autonomy and, because it was a small agency, there was a contender culture – we had to try very hard, and that struck a chord.

'Now my job is more to do with strategy; dealing with and planning advertising activity rather than buying. The best kick is to win a client, and the merger with Mediacom made us big enough to have real clout so that clients consider our pitch even if we're not the number one choice. Winning as an outsider is an amazing feeling, even more so because we have generated great team spirit. One of the most rewarding feelings for me is to see someone in the team develop and become a top-class planner.'

By comparison, although not necessarily by choice, Emma is a loner. Much as she may like to, it is impossible to develop a go-get-'em team spirit among a collection of workmen who come and go with such speed it is hard to engender much loyalty other than to the pay packet. Her employees mainly press buttons to produce kingpins and forgings that are now dressed and shaped by computer. Man-operated machinery such as lathes and capstans do exist in her factory in case of emergency, but they lie idle for lengthy periods. Savage Components has supported her family in a pleasant way of life for 40 years, but the Black Country, which existed under a blanket of yellowish-grey discharge for 200 years as the cradle of the world's heavy industry, is now practically a clean-air zone and the men who laboured in its foundries and factories – making everything metal, from washers to nuclear reactors – vanished one or two generations ago. Today, Emma and a few employers in similar businesses are the tail end of this leviathan, and sometimes she wonders if all the work and worry is worthwhile. But never forget those competitive instincts or the sheer joy of completion.

'I have gained three big customers since Dad died, which was vital because we were not breaking even then. We are producing king-pins, the fifth wheel coupling on trucks and trailers, after official approval following tests to destruction. It was a bit of a risk to do this, but having quality certificates gives me extra scope and we are now machining 1000 a month to go to Germany, and Dad would have been over the moon. The plan next year is to get up to 1500 kingpins and then 2000.

'We manufacture similar forgings for a Sheffield firm, but not in those quantities. I admit that a lot of my selling has been by good luck. I thought I would do it in a more professional way by taking on a sales guy, but I had to get rid of him because he did not bring me any new work, and now, while I do make attempts to sell to new customers, I find it has been much more viable to increase my ongoing work. Our biggest customer in Wrexham buys 80% of our output but I have big hopes of increasing it overall by 50–60%, producing cam rollers and pins for a company in Switzerland. This would require two shifts here and I have to think whether I want that.

'Ali and I try to control everything, and that might not be possible. Our annual turnover currently is £600,000–£700,000 and *what kills us is that my premises are rented. I realize now that when Dad sold the land to the supermarket he should have bought a site, not rented it. We are ploughing £40,000 a year into rent and that is very worrying. I have just finished paying for a magazine bar fitter at £80,000 and, because of depreciation, I haven't bought a new machine for years – everything has been second-hand, including the machining centre. We buy one-metre steel bars from this country, Spain and Czechoslovakia, and it just churns out all day long. Then the components go elsewhere for heat treatment, and finally to another processing plant, which gives them a salt-spray resistant film.'*

Keeping your head and your focus

Emma talks about steel bars with as much affection as she might about a pet dog. And she has a healthy disrespect for accountants, a useful trait in any entrepreneur.

'After Dad died, the accountant told me we were in a black hole. I said: "You are my accountant, don't knock me down; let me see what I can do. I am trying to keep going." He couldn't understand why I carried on after the supermarket deal. He thought I should close or sell. It's true that by keeping going I have eaten a little bit into the land profit and occasionally I do think of a cold sell. If someone approached me and said they would like to buy, it would be stupid to walk away. Business friends would encourage me to sell, I know that. But maybe I would be stupid.

'The bank is really good. I have a small overdraft facility but they are more than happy and have always been very encouraging. It helps that all my customers are responsible and pay on time. The accountant does all my figures for me and, because it is essential I know where I'm going, I keep in touch with him all the time. I know what I need to do monthly to be doing okay, and I project forward to see whether I am a few thousand short of break-even

point. I learned quite a lot about business management when I took a national certificate on a day-release course.

'When we started making kingpins, I met one of the forgers for the first time. Afterwards he sent me an e-mail in which he said he wanted to hug me because I was made of stern stuff. It's great – a lot my friends and business contacts look at me like that. I never look back and trash myself for making mistakes – they are just part of the learning curve. I am looking to buy a new factory, but it is a risk because the competition in engineering is growing, especially in India and Turkey where labour is so cheap. No one can be sure of the future of engineering in this country. It isn't a big money-maker. I know it is lovely doing what you want to do and I would love to think I could continue to take the business further, but there are easier ways to make money. This is bloody hard work.'

Neither Emma nor Karen is the type to surrender. If Emma were to, she would be opening up a new avenue within weeks. What they have had to give up – or have had give up on them – are boyfriends who fail to under-stand their motivation. This is an occupational hazard amongst women who refuse to devote themselves without restriction to men who think they must own unlimited hours of their undivided attention. Jacqueline Gold referred to this ego-condition several times, commenting that 'Guys think they are being diminished.' Karen says of her experience:

'Successful women are multi-taskers. I would love to have kids, but not doing so can be one of the sacrifices you have to make when you focus on your career. It's not really about finding the time; it's about being in the right situation. Several of my relationships have been affected, that's definite. Some men aren't happy with the competi-tion of long hours, or not being as successful or not having as much money. It all makes it difficult to maintain a normal relationship. Working at weekends is particularly hard for a boyfriend to come to terms with and, for me, it broke an affair. I think my current boy-friend is the right person; he wants children but he's younger. I went out for a long time with someone the same age and our incomes were disproportionate because this pays well. He did not like it.

There seems to be this macho thing with men who are older than I am – they think my role should be supporting them in their career, which is bizarre. Someone younger enjoys your success. Perhaps it's ego with the older ones: the men I meet are usually here at work so it is a certain type in this industry.'

Emma's boyfriends also fought unsuccessfully against her long hours, and she also had to forsake playing tennis for Warwickshire:

'County tennis took up a lot of time because there was a big social side to it. I'd go to a party, have a few drinks and, generally, live, eat and breathe it, and it all became too much to fit in with work, so I gave it up. I was shattered all the time from the hours I had to spend completing orders, sometimes until 2.00 a.m. I haven't been away for three years. I've worked all the bank holidays except Christmas, although I did manage a week off for the industrial shutdown.

'All this has caused a few problems in relationships. I split with one man, and another – well, I'm half back with him. They would both say: "Emma, all you seem to want to do is work, go home and go to bed – you don't seem to want to be with me." There was a bit of jealousy, too, because I would go out with a customer in the evening to talk about business and they would ask why I couldn't do it in working hours. It didn't help either that when we went out for a drink, I would want to be happy, talk a bit about work but they didn't wish to know. That caused some conflict. We had terrible rows.'

There have to be compensations, and for Emma these are in the pure satisfaction of seeing a job done:

'It's a challenge. I am a competitive person and the kick is thriving on stress. I have been brought up in industry. I just love making my stuff: love seeing it all on pallets, bagged up, on its way to Switzerland or Germany. We have been in this business for more than 40 years and we have a very good reputation all around the world. Yes, we are comparatively just a little shop, but it's great to be doing important work from it. I like being respected by firms and by my own staff

and, yes, I know that during a succession of employment tribunal cases immediately after Dad died, I found it hard. I threatened to quit loads of times, but on each occasion I said to myself: "They're not going to beat me."'

Looking ahead

For Karen, her biggest business thrill comes at the moment when the team she has put together pitches for a new account and wins it. But I don't think for a minute that she sees herself remaining as marketing director for very long. She is hugely ambitious and sees her colour as no disadvantage to progressing upwards. She has strong criticisms though:

'The advertising industry is perceived as more liberal and laid-back than most, and so there tends to be a 50/50 split between men and women, although not in board and executive jobs – a fact that I partly put down to the upper echelons being an old boys' network, rife with nepotism as well. Black people are few and far between, but it doesn't seem to me that I have been disadvantaged. I have come across sexism and chauvinism. I know you shouldn't have to, but I go out of way to prove people with those views as wrong. Many times I have seen the look of shock when I am introduced to media owners, creative agencies and clients. It just makes me smile; it's ridiculous. If I can act as a role model to women and black people, I would be delighted, although I am well aware that it shouldn't be necessary. In my case, I haven't been overlooked, but I know the higher you rise, the more difficult it is to make that next step.'

This braking process was referred to by Kate Hartigan, too. Indeed, she made the point that the more senior the position, the harder it was for a woman to be appointed. She thought a board might well question whether there was more of a risk with a woman than with a man, and possibly this was the reason why at major companies with huge balance sheets there were so few women directors – which is why rising with the business is often a quicker way to the top than moving around.

However, she laughed at her own experience when she was appointed finance director at Ina. The chief executive was down to the final two candidates, herself and a man, both capable, and she was offered the job because when he asked himself what would be the implications, he thought it would shake up the business a bit. With her skills, Karen would, I am sure, rise even more swiftly in local government or one of the utilities, but she may regard this as a softer option; territory that has already been inhabited, if not exactly conquered, by women. She has a bantering sense of humour – the natural recourse in her business – and inner drive and determination. In performance psychologist Alma Thomas's words she has 'the extra male genes that make her able to think like a man', an opinion confirmed by Karen's comment that the seven women on the Mediacom board all have 'quite masculine traits', herself included. She continued:

> 'I suppress my feminine side; it's silly, but I do – that's me, personally. I was brought up as a tomboy, like my sister. My MD jokes: "You're a spit and sawdust girl." Many women use their femininity to try to get where they want to be. That's fine; each to her own. Most of the senior directors are men, and if a woman perceives her chances are better if she is eye-candy, that's okay. I'm not pretty enough and wouldn't know how to do it. There are certain things some women need, which I park when I am at work. I swear with the boys. If someone swore at me, my natural reaction would be to do so back, probably with a better expletive. Our business is like that. I should add, however, that I can be quite diplomatic.'

Dealing with setbacks

So, for different reasons and to different audiences, Karen and Emma are both capable of swapping colourful language. I am not unknown for this ability, either. From earlier chapters, you will have gathered that I am interested in how women respond to setbacks or crises. I know from working in advertising that there can be many, many disappointments before the shining moments arrive. Here was Karen talking about it:

'Lots of times I have made new business pitches, and when I haven't won I always kick myself that I should have done x or y, but I always learn from my biggest mistakes. As sure as hell and, damn it, I don't make the same mistake again. You just have to pick yourself up because if you don't, if you feel depressed and a failure, you'll be a drain on everyone else. I do blame myself and think I'm not good enough, but it's no good beating up on myself, I know that – I just have to get on with it.

'I am not a naturally overt salesman at all, certainly not the easy-patter type, but I quickly understand a client's needs and the opportunity they present, matching what we can offer to their needs. I also have tenacity and will not easily give up. You can't afford to be offended in my business. A thick skin is needed because it is inevitable that you will be regularly told to piss off. Then it's important you are diplomatic and tell the client that you understand their needs and then go back later when something else arises. Stay on their radar – that's the message.

'I have noticed traits in some of the other women in this agency, where they will take on more and more because they don't want to be seen as weak. It's true of me, too, because when I'm compared with male colleagues, I don't want to feel I can't prove myself. In a male-dominated industry women don't like to be singled out as different or awkward. I am still only learning to say: "No, I can't do that." I am learning that if I can't answer a question, it's much more acceptable to be honest and reply: "I am not sure about the answer. I'll come back later with it," than to spout nonsense solely to be saying something. I think one of the differences between business-men and women is that women don't have the kind of ego that will dent. All human beings can't be expected to know everything at one point in time.'

Emma's equivalent of Karen's disappointment over failed sales pitches would be to miss out on lucrative contracts, but for someone with her responsibilities there are few experiences more worrying, and time-consuming, than the employment tribunal. It can shred the strongest of moral fibre. Emma had three cases in swift succession and admits she hated each episode:

> 'One guy who had been with us for six years said he suffered a hernia at the factory and claimed that my father, when he was alive, had noted it in the accident book. I told him this wasn't so because I knew he had got the hernia through putting up a fence in his back garden. He swore at me and then started throwing things around the shop floor, which is extremely dangerous. To be honest, I would have wrapped a hammer round his head, but I held off, thank goodness, and ordered him to leave and come back when he was calmer. When he did, I sacked him. We went through all legal processes and I won the case in the tribunal, but there were times when I thought I wouldn't be able to cope. My father wasn't there to fight his own battle and that made it very difficult.
>
> 'On another occasion, I had a solicitor's letter claiming unfair dismissal. This particular guy was a troublemaker and I had gone through all the processes for sacking. I went out of my way to find out a bit more about him and discovered that he had stolen an old lady's purse when he had his little boy with him. I went to his solicitor and asked him: "Who are they going to believe, me or this guy caught on camera nicking an old lady's purse?" They settled out of court.
>
> 'I am sure some of these guys were conspiring to try it on with me just after Dad died, because in the third case one of them said the state of the factory had brought on asthma, which was ridiculous because you could eat your dinner off the floor. In the end, he backed off. I have one at the moment who is trying it on, perhaps because I'm a woman, I don't know. He does his job, he's never late, but verbally he's a male chauvinist. I had a general manager, a customer, at the factory and I asked this guy to show him how to do a particular process. He replied that it wasn't his job to show customers how to do things; it was mine. There was a showdown after that and I gave him a verbal warning. He should have been sacked but you have to go through such a rigmarole to do that, despite all the grief some people give.

'My size of business just can't afford passengers and it upsets me when I have to sack people, but I have to – and in the best way I can. I have to listen to such rubbish on the floor. One lad – he's only 19 and has three children – keeps taking time off or saying he has to go home in the middle of work to look after the kids. I want to show compassion, so I pulled him into my office and said: "We are carrying you. This is how many days you have had off. I know you have problems and I have tried to be understanding but unless you sort yourself I am going to have to find someone new. I run a small ship and everyone has a key job: your shoes need to be filled." He came back the next day and said he was really sorry, that he felt as if he had been taking the mickey. I have given him a bit more time, but he has had chances and pay rises and he hasn't been giving me any encouragement. I was trying to be compassionate and tough in the same breath.

'Once I've had enough I can get a bit angry. I try not to be emotional but can't help it sometimes. I would regard selling up as my failure, but then there would not be much point in breaking my back just to be losing and paying the wages.'

Pioneering women

In many ways, Emma is more of a pioneer than Karen, and quite possibly she is one of a rare breed of boss-women who will become extinct. This is partly because owning and running a steel works from the shop floor isn't seen as a desirable career path for a young woman, but also because our engineering industry is in steep decline. Karen's business is extremely healthy and women are proving in all forms of the media that they are at least the equal of men. Her climb so far is only exceptional because of her background. That, of course, should be immaterial, and I pray that it will be within a few generations. So what is her style?

'Mediacom has 300 staff now, but because we grew as a small business we still think in that way. We are the non-corporate corporate agency and so we still think as if we are a contender. It's a very open *forum, not office-political, and if you have an opinion we want to hear it even though it might upset someone.*

'As a person to work for, or with, my team know I am a perfection-ist and challenging. I have had people come on board and it hasn't worked out and I have had to tell them that and they left. That's a part of being manager. You have to be businesslike and not dress it up. You have to be factual and honest, which can come across as cold. I am not insensitive or unsympathetic but when I am at work, I am at work, not at play. If someone has a problem, I am approach-able. I take time to give direction, but if something is not sinking in and taking lots of time then that is something we have to discuss further. I try to be sympathetic with personal problems and I think women are much better at dealing with these. Some male bosses don't want to hear personal things and I have had bosses who com-ment: "Women are more trouble than they are worth," which is an appalling thing to say.

'It is very important to have a sense of humour and I enjoy banter, perhaps because I am not very hierarchical. When I was a junior planner-buyer I liked an environment with approachable people who would sometimes have a laugh with me. There have to be boundaries, though, and when someone is taking the piss you have to stop it straight away. I have been here eight years now and when-ever I have begun to think I was becoming a bit bored, they have thrown something else at me.'

Karen has come a long way, but she sticks to her roots. She goes to Barbados regularly because she has already bought a home there. 'It's three bedrooms and two bathrooms, in St James, and I rent it out when I'm not there. I have an eye for a bargain,' she says.

Just how exceptional Karen and Emma are in their competitiveness, I don't know, but psychologist Alma Thomas, who helped many women athletes, has an insight: 'Many women find it difficult to be competitive in the entrepreneurial way because they think it's a nasty thing to be and be seen to be.' She continues:

'I have run workshops on it and I explain that if there are eight people on the line, one of them has to win. To induce that kind of thinking pattern in women is not an easy thing to do because they are not brought up or trained to be that way. There's nothing to stop them saying: "Yes, I can do that and I don't need to be like a man to do that." It's about acknowledging who you are. I don't like women copying men because they see them as being successful. Women have their own way of doing things and just because their ways are not the same as men's doesn't mean they are not successful. One of the things in sport is that women don't need special treatment; they need different treatment. We need to give ourselves enough confidence to say: "I'm going to do it my way."'

Karen and Emma are doing it their way. And so can you.

Key lessons

- *The art of being successful is to get yourself into the winning habit. With a bit of luck, it will become second nature.*
- *You will undoubtedly have to deal with setbacks and crises, whatever your chosen career path. It's a normal part of daily life, and the way you deal with these moments will determine where you go from there, so be prepared to roll your sleeves up and find a way through.*
- *Being competitive is all part of the game. By following the lessons you have read in this book, and staying ultra-competitive at all times, you stand a fantastic chance of making your dreams into reality.*

epilogue: some final words of advice

In many aspects, a woman starting up in business is no different from a man. This may explain the absence from the Internet of advice aimed directly at women, although I think it also emphasizes the apathy of government, commerce and industry in directing information towards us as potential business high-risers. This is not a criticism I would necessarily aim at the public services, in which, figures show, women are far more likely to rise to senior executive positions. I still allow myself an inward smile, however, at the strange preponderance of women in management services in health and social work compared with those in production businesses: the total is 73%, against 6% in production.

This is a mild digression. More pertinently, there are one or two excellently informative packages for anyone, whether a man or woman, who wishes to become self-employed. In particular, I would recommend the Self-Employment Kit produced by Law Pack Publishing Ltd, 76–89 Alscot Road, London SE1 3AW (www.lawpack.co.uk). The Femail website (www.femail.com) is sometimes helpful with general issues. You will find dozens of websites aimed at Americans and, very occasionally, these are useful too.

My general advice to a woman with the desire to be independent in business is to do the homework thoroughly before branching out. Your ideas may be brilliant and workable but, if they cannot be sustained by sound planning, you will burn out, and quickly. It may well be that you have explored some of the potential for the idea by working in your spare time, but while this will give you a basis to set up alone, it is important to realize that, when you do so, there will be no source of cash from an employer: everything must be self-generated. You must also take a close look at your own personality and ask, of yourself and of others who might know, whether you are cut out to start and run a business, bearing in mind that it doesn't so much fit into your lifestyle as take it over. Think about this for at least a month, and try to discover examples of people who have been successful, and the reasons why. There is great security in knowing what you wish to do and how to get there, and, although it may not be the most engrossing thing you do, keeping monthly records on the whole business is, I think, essential. Money you spend on seeking an accountant's assistance will not be wasted, and neither will a close relationship with a bank.

There are many lists of dos and don'ts, but never forget that if you don't invoice, you don't get paid. Keep a ledger and don't let it get out of date. Prepare a business plan, and perhaps the easiest way to do this is to view it as though you are trying to attract a loan or grant from an outside source. This will encourage you to be positive without going overboard. Remember the saying: Fail to prepare, prepare to fail. Prepare your business plan and stick to it!

I wish you good fortune with your ventures.

Index